GERMAN BOMBER AIRCRAFT OF WORLD WAR II
1939–45

GERMAN BOMBER AIRCRAFT OF WORLD WAR II
1939–45

THOMAS NEWDICK

BOOKS

Reprinted in 2023

Copyright © 2020 Amber Books Ltd

All rights reserved. No part of this publication may be reproduced, stored in a retrieval system, or transmitted in any form or by any means, electronic, mechanical, photocopying, recording, or otherwise, without prior written permission of the copyright holder.

Published by Amber Books Ltd
United House
London N7 9DP
United Kingdom
www.amberbooks.co.uk
Facebook: amberbooks
Instagram: amberbooksltd
Twitter: @amberbooks
Pinterest: amberbooksltd

ISBN: 978-1-78274-971-4

Editor: Michael Spilling
Designer: Andrew Easton
Picture research: Terry Forshaw

Printed in China

Contents

Introduction	6
Bombers	8
Ground-Attack and Reconnaissance Aircraft	52
Transports and Gliders	74
Seaplanes and Maritime Aircraft	90
Helicopters	116
Glossary	122
Index	124
Picture Credits	128

Introduction

While dominated by the Luftwaffe's bombers, this volume includes the major reconnaissance, transport and maritime types – including seaplanes – developed and fielded by Germany during World War II, as well as some of the world's first military helicopters.

The Luftwaffe pioneered the use of aircraft in close air support and army cooperation roles – most famously with the Junkers Ju 87 Stuka – although it's worth noting that, as the war progressed, the boundary between fighter and ground-attack aircraft became increasingly blurred. For the purposes of this book, ground-attack aircraft are defined as those that were originally designed for this role.

In contrast with the Allied air arms, when Hitler embarked on his subjugation of Europe, the Luftwaffe's role was largely confined to providing air support for the German Wehrmacht, with little emphasis laid upon the use of strategic bombers, plans for such a force having been abandoned in 1937.

When Germany's fortunes changed – starting with the inability to crush Britain's Royal Air Force in summer 1940 – a progressive reassessment was carried out to address the Luftwaffe's capacity to take the air war beyond the English Channel. The 'Night Blitz' of 1940–41 represented an unpremeditated use of relatively small bombers for strategic purposes and achieved far more than had proved possible by day.

But the proliferation of battlefronts from 1941 onwards forced a dispersal

Seen here on a makeshift landing strip in Libya in June 1942 alongside a Messerschmitt Bf 110, the Junkers Ju 52/3m proved crucial in the movement of supplies and materiel in difficult terrain and extreme weather conditions.

INTRODUCTION

A navigator/bombardier examines a map during a mission from the extensively glazed 'greenhouse' nose of a Heinkel He 111 bomber.

of German bombers and other offensive aircraft away from the Atlantic coast; as a result of growing demands for fighters and ground-attack aircraft across multiple theatres, the Luftwaffe's offensive force began to decline in strength and relative quality.

Inevitably, the mounting losses suffered by the Luftwaffe on the Eastern Front and in the Mediterranean (as Allied strength increased everywhere) deprived the Luftwaffe of air superiority over the land battle. The traditional weapon of *blitzkrieg*, the Junkers Ju 87, could no longer attack at will, being faced by formidable fighter opposition almost everywhere. Yet in the absence of a more advanced replacement, the Germans were forced to persevere with the Ju 87, and thereby suffered heavy losses.

Maritime operations

Another important task of the Luftwaffe was attacks against coastal shipping, and the incessant vigil against submarines, roles that employed both adaptations of bombers and transports, the latter category perhaps reaching its zenith with the Focke-Wulf Fw 200 Condor. The Dornier Do 217 and Junkers Ju 88 medium bombers also proved effective in anti-shipping strikes, especially against the Allied North Cape convoys, in which the Heinkel He 111 also participated.

On the transport side, Germany used aircraft to deliver forces direct to the battlefield from the air: one of the first expressions of airmobile warfare. As well as paratroopers, Germany developed a new method of transporting soldiers by means of towed gliders, and both methods were put into action in the opening months of the war, before being applied to the large action in Crete in 1941.

For duties involving covert operations, such as transport of agents, rescue of shot-down airmen from enemy territory and other missions involving use of remote or confined sites, the lightplane was the obvious solution. Of all the aircraft employed in these tasks, perhaps none was better than the Fieseler Fi 156 *Storch*: its agility became legendary, even after the first helicopters had become an effective component of the world's arsenals.

BOMBERS

At the outbreak of war in September 1939, the Luftwaffe's bombing arm comprised excellent medium bombers (the Dornier Do 17, Heinkel He 111 and Junkers Ju 88) that were regarded as adequate for the task of subjugating Europe, a job that was expected to take no more than three years.

This chapter includes the following aircraft:

- Heinkel He 111
- Junkers Ju 86
- Dornier Do 17 and Dornier Do 215
- Dornier 217
- Junkers Ju 88
- Heinkel He 177
- Messerschmitt Me 264
- Junker Ju 188
- Arado Ar 234 *Blitz*
- Fieseler Fi 103R *Reichenberg*

A Heinkel He 111 bomber flies over the East End docks area of London, Autumn 1940.

BOMBERS

Heinkel He 111

The He 111 began life as a commercial airliner design but found its niche as a medium bomber, remaining the standard type in service with the Luftwaffe at the outbreak of World War II.

The initial prototype was the He 111 V1, the configuration of which was based on a scaled-up He 70 mailplane. It was powered by a pair of 492kW (660hp) BMW VI 6,0Z inverted-Vee engines and completed a first flight on 24 February 1935.

Civilian prototypes

The second and third prototypes, the He 111 V1 and V2, introduced a wing of reduced span and were completed as a 10-seat civilian transport and a bomber respectively.

Another civilian prototype, the He 111 V4, was next to fly and was demonstrated in public on 10 January 1936. A pre-production batch of six He 111C aircraft was completed on the basis of the V4 and entered service with Lufthansa in the same year. A variety of different powerplants were used, including BMW 132 radials.

Meanwhile, work continued on a bomber version, but the performance of the He 111 V2 was judged disappointing, with a cruising speed of 270km/h (168mph) due to the engines' limited power output and the weight of the various military equipment. The He 111 V5 prototype was intended to address the deficiencies of the initial bomber iteration and served as the pattern aircraft for the He 111B – the initial production series of the bomber. The He 111 V5 completed its maiden flight in early 1936 and incorporated an uprated powerplant of two 746kW (1000hp) Daimler-Benz DB 600A inverted-Vee engines.

The revised aircraft quickly demonstrated great potential and additional production capacity was set up in advance of the B-series. The first deliveries of He 111B-1 aircraft were made to 1./KG 154 at Fassberg in late 1936. In advance of this, however, a small run of 10 pre-production He 111A-0 bombers had been completed; they proved so disappointing in tests that they were sold to China. While the He 111B-1 was powered by two 656kW (880hp) DB 600Cs, the He 111B-2 that followed utilized the 708kW (950hp) DB 600CG engines.

Spanish Civil War

From February 1937, a total of 30 He 111B-1s were delivered to the Legion Condor in Spain. After this combat debut, the He 111 became the spearhead of the Luftwaffe's bomber

Heinkel He 111B-1

Wearing the civilian registration D-ARAU, this He 111B-1 was based in Germany during November–December 1936. It wears the typical interwar three-colour splinter camouflage scheme.

Heinkel He 111B-1

Weight (Maximum take-off) 8200kg (18,080lb)
Dimensions Length: 16.4m (53ft 9in), Wingspan: 22.6m (74ft 2in), Height: 3.4m (11ft 2in)
Powerplant Two 656kW (880hp) Daimler-Benz DB 600C inverted V-12 engines
Speed 368km/h (229mph)
Range 1060km (660 miles) (maximum fuel)
Ceiling 7000m (22,965ft)
Crew 5
Armament Three 7.92mm (0.31in) MG 15 machine guns; 1500kg (3310lb) bombload

BOMBERS

formations in the early years of World War II. However, the type soon proved vulnerable to fighter interception and as the Junkers Ju 88 arrived in numbers, the Heinkel bomber was increasingly switched to night operations.

Heinkel He 111D

A first attempt to boost the performance of the bomber resulted in the He 111D with a pair of DB 600Ga engines and with the auxiliary wing radiators removed. In the event, production was abandoned in favour of the He 111E, introduced in response to a shortage of the DB 600 engines. Instead, the E-series was powered by the 746kW (1000hp) Junkers Jumo 211A-1 engines, which had been trialled in an earlier example of the He 111D-0.

The pre-production He 111E-0 prototype featured an increased bombload and was followed by the series-production He 111E-1, which began to be delivered in 1938. Next in line were the He 111E-2 and E-3, which featured a further increased bombload, and the He 111E-5 with an auxiliary fuel tank in the fuselage for an increase in combat radius.

A new, straight-tapered wing was introduced in the He 111G, which also found employment on the He 111F. The He 111F-1 was first supplied to Turkey, which received 24 examples. As well as the new wing, these incorporated

Heinkel He 111E-1

Seen as it appeared during the Spanish Civil War in 1938, this He 111E-1 was operated by Kampfgruppe 88 as part of the Condor Legion fighting on behalf of the Spanish Nationalists.

Jumo 211A-3 engines. The similar He 111F-4 was produced for the Luftwaffe, which took delivery of 40 examples in 1938. Examples of the F-series were also converted for torpedo carriage, resulting in the He 111J, with 708kW (950hp) DB 600CG engines.

When allied with the He 111C, the straight-tapered wing produced the He 111G-1 variant and successive subvariants differed in their choice of powerplant. The He 111G-3 featured 656kW (880hp) BMW 132Dc radial

Heinkel He 111E-1

Weight (Maximum take-off) 10,300kg (22,707lbs)
Dimensions Length: 16.4m (53ft 9in), Wingspan: 22.6m (74ft 2in), Height: 3.4m (11ft 2in)
Powerplant Two 746kW (1000hp) Junkers Jumo 211A-1 V-12 piston engines
Speed 436km/h (271mph)
Range 2100km (1305 miles) (maximum fuel)
Ceiling 6500m (21,300ft)
Crew 5
Armament Three 7.92mm (0.31in) MG 15 machine guns; 1700kg (3748lb) bombload

Armourers load two practice LT F5b torpedoes on to an He 111H-6. Although mainly used as a bomber, this variant achieved spectacular success in the anti-shipping role while operating with KG 26 in Norway.

Heinkel He 111P-2
Kampfgeschwader 55 operated this He 111P-2 on the 'Night Blitz' nocturnal raids against the United Kingdom in late 1940 and early 1941, flying from Dreux and Villacoublay in France.

engines, while the He 111G-4 was powered by 671kW (900hp) DB 600G units. The DB 600Ga engine was the chosen powerplant of the He 111G-5, four examples of which were supplied to Turkey.

Heinkel He 111P redesign
In 1939 the He 111 was subject to a major redesign, re-emerging as the He 111H and He 111P that were developed in parallel, the two sharing a revised fuselage with the original stepped cockpit replaced by an asymmetric glazed cockpit and nose.

The P-series was tested in the form of the He 111P-0, with a ventral gondola with a prone position and a powerplant of two 858kW (1150hp) DB 601Aa engines. Deliveries of the initial-production He 111P-1 began in late 1939. Changes to the radio equipment characterized the He 111P-2, while the He 111P-3 featured dual controls for training pilots. The He 111P-4 standardized on a five-man crew and also added additional defensive armour and armament.

The He 111P-6, meanwhile, was powered by 876kW (1175hp) DB 601N engines and had its 2000kg (4409lb) bombload stowed vertically in the fuselage. Examples of the H-6 were converted as glider tugs under the He 111P-6/R2 designation.

Heinkel He 111H
More prolific than the P-series was the He 111H, in which the He 111H-0 and H-1 were essentially similar to the

Heinkel He 111H-1
Operating from France in 1940, this He 111H-1 was assigned to Kampfgeschwader 1.

Heinkel He 111P-2
Weight (Maximum take-off) 12,570kg (27,712lb)
Dimensions Length: 16.4m (53ft 9in), Wingspan: 22.6m (74ft 2in), Height: 3.4m (11ft 2in)
Powerplant Two 858kW (1150hp) Daimler-Benz DB 601Aa inverted V-12 engines
Speed 475km/h (295mph)
Range 2100km (1305 miles) (maximum fuel)
Ceiling 6500m (21,300ft)
Crew 5
Armament Five 7.92mm (0.31in) MG 15 machine guns; 2000kg (4400lb) bombload

---

Heinkel He 111H-1
Weight (Maximum take-off) 14,000kg (30,865lb)
Dimensions Length: 16.4m (53ft 9in), Wingspan: 22.6m (74ft 2in), Height: 3.4m (11ft 2in)
Powerplant Two 753kW (1100hp) Junkers Jumo 211A V-12 piston engines
Speed 436km/h (271mph)
Range 2300km (1400 miles) (maximum fuel)
Ceiling 8500m (27,890ft)
Crew 5
Armament Three 7.92mm (0.31in) MG 15 machine guns; eight SC 250 250kg (550lb) or 32 SC 50 50kg (110lb) bombs

BOMBERS

Heinkel He 111H-6
Weight (Maximum take-off) 14,000kg (30,865lb)
Dimensions Length: 16.4m (53ft 9in), Wingspan: 22.6m (74ft 2in), Height: 3.4m (11ft 2in)
Powerplant Two 990kW (1320hp) Junkers Jumo 211F-1 V-12 piston engines
Speed 436km/h (271mph)
Range 2300km (1400 miles) (maximum fuel)
Ceiling 6500m (21,300ft)
Crew 5
Armament Up to seven 7.92mm (0.31in) MG 15 or MG 81 machine guns (two nose, one dorsal, two side, two ventral); 2000kg (4400lb) bombload in main internal bomb bay

He 111P-2, but with 753kW (1100hp) Jumo 211A engines. In 1939 the He 111H-3 appeared, which included up to seven MG 15 defensive machine guns. The He 111H-4 had Jumo 211D-1 engines and a pair of external racks for bombs or torpedoes; the He 111H-5 was similar but with increased fuel capacity.

The addition of Jumo 211F-1 engines produced the He 111H-6, also featuring a machine gun in the tail cone. In order to combat barrage balloons, the He 111H-3 and H-5 were retrofitted with cable fenders, becoming He 111H-8 aircraft. Of the H-8s, many were subsequently converted as glider tugs (He 111H-8/R2). Another wartime revision was the He 111H-10 night-bomber for raids on Britain, with reduced armament and balloon cable-cutters on the wing leading edges.

Variants

Armament revisions were introduced in the He 111H-11 and H-11/R1, while the He 111H-12 and H-15 were equipped to launch missiles. The He 111H-14 was a dedicated pathfinder version, followed by another major production model, the He 111H-16, which was similar to the H-11, but

Heinkel He 111H-6
This He 111H-6 of Gefechtsverband (Combat Formation) Kulmey flew from Immola Airfield in Finland, July 1944.

Heinkel He 111H-16
Weight (Maximum take-off) 14,000kg (30,865lb)
Dimensions Length: 16.4m (53ft 9in), Wingspan: 22.6m (74ft 2in), Height: 3.4m (11ft 2in)
Powerplant Two 1000kW (1340hp) Jumo 211F-2 V-12 piston engines
Speed 436km/h (271mph)
Range 2300km (1400 miles) (maximum fuel)
Ceiling 8500m (27,890ft)
Crew 5
Armament One 13mm (0.51in) MG 131, four 7.92mm (0.31in) MG 81Zs, two 7.92mm (0.31in) MG 15 machine guns; 3250kg (7165lb) bombload

Heinkel He 111H-16
Assigned to the *Stab* (Staff) flight of II./Kampfgeschwader 53, this He 111H-16 was flying from Oslufwejo, southern Russia, between July and September 1943.

BOMBERS

Fuel Tanks
The wing contained two 700 litre (154 Imp gal) fuel tanks. Reserve fuel tanks were between the outer spars. The He 111 used the inner fuel tanks, closest to the wing root, first.

Heinkel He 111H-22

Weight (Maximum take-off) 14,000kg (30,865lb)

Dimensions Length: 16.4m (53ft 9in), Wingspan: 22.6m (74ft 2in), Height: 3.4m (11ft 2in)

Powerplant Two 1007kW (1350hp) Junkers Jumo 211F inverted V-12 engines

Speed 436km/h (271mph)

Range 1950km (1212 miles)

Ceiling 6700m (21,980ft)

Crew 5

Armament One 20mm (0.79in) MG FF cannon in nose, one 13mm (0.51in) MG 131 gun in dorsal position, two 7.92mm (0.31in) MG 15s in rear gondola, two 7.92mm (0.31in) MG 15s in each of two beam positions; one Fieseler Fi 103 flying bomb

Fieseler Fi 103 Flying Bomb
Also known as the V-1 Flying Bomb ('Vengeance Weapon 1'), and 'Doodlebug' to the Allies, the Fi 103 was an early cruise missile. It used a pulse jet for power. The missile was launched from beneath the starboard wing.

BOMBERS

Defensive Armament
The He 111H-22 included a single 13mm (0.51in) MG 131 in the dorsal gun turret as a defence against fighter attacks from above.

Crew
The standard crew for the He 111 was five: a pilot, who sat in the glazed section; a navigator/bombardier, who sat in the nose; a radio operator/dorsal gunner; and two further gunners, who operated machine guns in the beams and ventral gondola, which was known to the crew as the *Stertebett* ('death bed').

Heinkel He 111H-22 (with Fieseler Fi 103)
Following experiments at Peenemünde, the German secret weapons establishment, in 1943, several Heinkel 111s were modified to carry a Feiseler Fi 103 (V-1) missile. The type was assigned to the newly formed III Gruppe, Kampfgeschwader (KG) 3, which became operational at Venlo and Gilze-Rijn in the Netherlands in July 1944. By August 1944, III./KG 3 had launched 300 V-1s against London. Redesignated II./KG 53 in October 1944, the unit had around 100 aircraft committed to V-1 flying bomb attacks against England. By January 1945, when operations ceased, the unit had lost 77 aircraft, mainly at the hands of RAF Mosquito night fighters, for which the lumbering combination was easy prey.

15

BOMBERS

Heinkel He 111H-20

Flown by 9./Kampfgeschwader 44, this He 111H-20 was based at Breslau in March 1945.

able to carry a 3250kg (7165lb) bombload with the aid of rocket-assisted take-off gear.

Subvariants were the He 111H-16/R1 with revolving dorsal turret, He 111H-16/R2 with rigid bar for towing gliders and the He 111H-16/R3 pathfinder. Another pathfinder, the He 111H-18, featured exhaust flame-dampers. As a military transport, the H-series was completed in the form of the He 111H-20/R1 with provision for 16 paratroopers. Derivatives included the He 111H-20/R2 night-bomber/glider tug; H-20/R3 with additional armour protection; and the H-20/R4, which could carry 20 50kg (110lb) SC 50 bombs.

Once the He 111H-20/R3 was fitted with 1305kW (1750hp) Jumo 213E-1 engines and two-stage superchargers, it became the He 111H-21 (or He 111 H-22 missile-carrier). Last of the line was the He 111H-23, another paratrooper transport, with 1324kW (1776hp) Jumo 213A-1 engines.

The most radical departure from the original bomber was the He 111Z (*Zwilling*, or twin), which combined two He 111H-6 airframes via a new common wing centre section carrying a fifth Jumo 211F-2 engine. Two prototypes and 10 production He 111Z-1 aircraft were built to transport the Me 321 Gigant transport glider.

Multipurpose aircraft

By the end of the war, therefore, the He 111 had served in roles as diverse as missile launching, torpedo-bombing, pathfinding and glider-towing, while transport variants played a key role in supporting and supplying beleaguered Wehrmacht troops at Stalingrad between November 1942 and February 1943.

Total production amounted to more than 7300 aircraft by the time the last aircraft was completed in autumn 1944.

Heinkel He 111H-20

Weight (Maximum take-off) 14,000kg (30,865lb)
Dimensions Length: 16.4m (53ft 9in), Wingspan: 22.6m (74ft 2in), Height: 3.4m (11ft 2in)
Powerplant Two 1350kW (1750hp) Jumo 213E-1 V-12 piston engines
Speed 436km/h (271mph)
Range 2300km (1400 miles) (maximum fuel)
Ceiling 8500m (27,890ft)
Crew 5
Armament Three 13mm (0.51in) MG 131s, two 7.92mm (0.31in) MG 81Zs, two 7.92mm (0.31in) MG 15 machine guns; 3250kg (7165lb) bombload

Heinkel He-111s undergo mass production in a German aircraft factory, October 1940.

Junkers Ju 86

The Ju 86 began life as a 10-seat airliner and a four-seat bomber, both of which were designed around a pair of the new Junkers Jumo 205 diesel engines.

These motors were not available, however, for the first prototype Ju 86abl that took to the air in 1934 with Siemens AM 9 radials. While the first prototype was a bomber, the second, Ju 86bal, was outfitted as a transport, with the planned Jumo 205C diesels. The third prototype, another bomber, was completed with the same engines as the first before later adding Jumo 205Cs.

Despite the disappointing performance exhibited by the three prototypes, work continued with the Ju 86 V4 fourth (commercial) and V5 fifth (bomber) prototypes, and 13 Ju 86A-0 pre-production bombers were followed by deliveries of the initial-production Ju 86A-1 to the Luftwaffe from February 1936. Meanwhile, seven pre-production civilian Ju 86B-0 aircraft began to be delivered to Swissair in April that year. The refined Ju 86C-1 was provided to Deutsche Lufthansa, which took six examples with Jumo 205C diesels.

Export versions

The next bomber derivative, the Ju 86D-1 with improved Jumo 205Cs, was delivered to the Condor Legion in Spain, but was judged inferior to the Heinkel He 111 also in theatre.

While the Luftwaffe was less than impressed with the D series, the Junkers design went on to win export orders from South Africa and Sweden, in the form of the Ju 86K-1, and Saab built further examples under licence.

Meanwhile, Hungary received the Ju 86K-2, while the Ju 86K-6 was completed for Chile and Portugal. Sweden's Ju 86K-4 was similar to the K-1 but featured Bristol Pegasus III radial engines and served under the local B 3A designation, while the B 3B covered K-1 equivalents powered by Swedish-made Pegasus XIII engines. The Ju 86K-13 subvariant was a Swedish-built bomber with either Swedish or Polish-made Pegasus powerplants.

Junkers Ju 86E

The Ju 86E was then developed as an improvement over the D series, and the initial Ju 86E-1 was re-engined with BMW 132P radials that provided much greater reliability; the

Junkers Ju 86D-1

The Ju 86 included a retractable gondola on the underside of the fuselage, where a single machine gun provided defensive armament.

Junkers Ju 86D-1

Weight (Maximum take-off) 8200kg (18,078lb)
Dimensions Length: 16.46m (54ft), Wingspan: 22.50m (73ft 10in), Height: 5.06m (16ft 7in)
Powerplant Two 600kW (447hp) Junkers Jumo 205C-4 six-cylinder engines
Speed 420km/h (260mph)
Range 1500km (932 miles)
Ceiling 12,800m (42,000ft)
Crew 2
Armament Three 7.92mm (0.31in) machine guns (nose, dorsal and ventral positions); 800kg (1764lb) bombload

subsequent Ju 86E-2 featured uprated BMW 132Ns.

Work continued to improve the basic design, and the final 40 Ju 86Es were thus completed as Ju 86G-1 aircraft with round glazed noses. The last of these was finished in 1938.

High-altitude bomber

The Ju 86's fortunes changed in 1939, however, when two Ju 86Ds were converted as prototypes for a high-altitude version, with Jumo 207 engines and a pressurized cabin. The success of these resulted in orders for the Ju 86P-1 bomber and the Ju 86P-2 reconnaissance aircraft, which could reach a ceiling of around 12,800m (42,000ft). Once a high-aspect ratio wing was added, these aircraft became the Ju 86R-1 for reconnaissance and the Ju 86R-2 high-altitude bombers respectively, but only a few of these saw service.

The R-series demonstrated excellent high-altitude performance, one example attaining a height of 14,440m (47,250ft).

Meanwhile, the proposed Ju 86R-3 with supercharged Jumo 208 engines was abandoned, as was the Ju 186 four-engine high-altitude bomber and six-engine Ju 286, intended for the same role.

Junkers Ju 86 aircraft stand in a row during a training exercise in 1939. Although an advanced bomber for its time, it was found to be unreliable in service.

Dornier Do 17 and Dornier Do 215

The Dornier Do 17 emerged from an original Deutsche Lufthansa requirement for a high-speed six-passenger mailplane drafted in 1933.

Dornier's response was a shoulder-wing, all-metal monoplane with a powerplant comprising two 492kW (660hp) BMW VI engines. In 1934 a total of three prototypes were completed – the first of these, the Do 17 V1, took to the air for the first time that autumn. The same year the carrier undertook an evaluation, before rejecting the design on account of its slender fuselage that limited passenger accommodation.

All three of the prototypes (Do 17 V1 having been joined by V2 and V3) were handed back to Dornier, but the company saw the military potential of the aircraft and followed up with a fourth prototype, the Do 17 V4, that introduced twin vertical tail surfaces for greater directional stability and a shortened fuselage lacking the cabin glazing of the previous prototypes. Internal changes included provision for a radio operator's position in place of the passenger compartment and the addition of a weapons bay in the lower fuselage, beginning immediately to the rear of the front wing spar. The revised Do 17 V4 took to the air in summer 1935.

The next aircraft, the fifth, included an alternative powerplant based on the 641kW (860hp) Hispano-Suiza 12Ybrs, and while the sixth was basically similar to the V4, the seventh added defensive armament in the form of a 7.92mm (0.31in) MG 15 machine gun in a dorsal blister. Until this point, it had been assumed that the aircraft's speed would protect it from fighter interception, but by now it was clear that some form of defensive firepower would be a necessity.

The tenth and final prototype added yet another new powerplant, the 559kW (750hp) BMW VI 7,3 high-compression engine and was used for development trials. As it was, the Do 17 V9 served as the pattern for the production aircraft and featured further refinements in the form of enlarged nose glazing with optically flat panels, additional glazing on the starboard side of the nose, improved defensive blister and enlarged vertical tail surfaces.

Dornier Do 17E-1

As introduced to series production, the Do 17E-1 version was based on the ninth prototype standard and was intended for use as a medium bomber with provision for a 500kg (1102lb) bombload (increased to 750kg/1653lb for short-range missions), while the Do 17E-2 was a reconnaissance aircraft. Both types made their operational

---

Dornier Do 17E-1
Weight (Maximum take-off) 7040kg (15,520lb)
Dimensions Length: 16.25m (53ft 3in), Wingspan: 18m (59ft), Height: 4.32m (14ft 2in)
Powerplant Two 559kW (750hp) BMW VI-7,3 piston engines
Speed 355km/h (220mph)
Range 500km (310 miles)
Ceiling 5100m (16,730ft)
Crew 4
Armament Three 7.92mm (0.31in) MG 15 machine guns; 500kg (1102lb) bombload

---

Dornier Do 17E-1

Assigned to an unidentified training unit around late 1939, this is an example of the Do 17E-1 initial series production version. Note the combination of four-digit code SA+HN and individual aircraft number '26', plus three-tone, upper surface splinter scheme.

BOMBERS

debut during the Spanish Civil War, where they arrived in 1937, the Do 17E-1 having been introduced to service with the I. Gruppen of Kampfgeschwader 153 and 155 earlier the same year. Additional units were also re-equipped with the new bomber the same year, including both II. and III./KG 153 and II. and III./KG 155 (although the latter was soon re-designated as KG 158). The type also served with KG 252 and KG 255.

The Do 17F-1 was the next reconnaissance version to enter production and featured two cameras as well as increased internal fuel capacity. Both the Do 17E-1 and F-1 shared the same defensive armament of two trainable MG 15 machine guns, firing rearwards from the dorsal and ventral hatch positions.

Dornier Do 17F-1
Croatian-operated Do 17F serial 0313, as it appeared around 1943. This aircraft defected to the Yugoslav partisans in November that year and was then destroyed in an air raid by a Luftwaffe Heinkel He 46.

Export model

The Do 17K version was developed for export in order to meet a Yugoslav requirement and was powered by two 731kW (980hp) Gnome-Rhône 14N1/2 engines. Licenced production was undertaken in Yugoslavia by the Drzavna Fabrika Aviona at Kraljevo. It was produced in three subvariants: the Do 17ZKb-1 bomber, plus the Do 17Ka-2 and Do 17Ka-3 reconnaissance aircraft with secondary bombing and attack capability. At least 70 of the K-series were built, of which

Dornier Do 17F-1
Weight (Maximum take-off) 7040kg (15,520lb)
Dimensions Length: 16.25m (53ft 3in), Wingspan: 18m (59ft), Height: 4.32m (14ft 2in)
Powerplant Two 559kW (750hp) BMW VI-7,3 piston engines
Speed 355km/h (220mph)
Range 500km (310 miles)
Ceiling 5100m (16,730ft)
Crew 4
Armament Three 7.92mm (0.31in) MG 15 machine guns; provision for 500kg (1102lb) bombload; two cameras along with six ejector tubes for flashlight cartridges

Seen in the winter of 1941/42, a Dornier Do 17Z from 7. Staffel III./KG 3 is bombed-up by traditional methods on the Eastern Front. The unit converted to the Junkers Ju 88 early in 1942.

20 were manufactured in Germany and the remainder in Yugoslavia.

A proposed pathfinder version was the Do 17L, two prototypes being produced powered by a pair of 671kW (900hp) Bramo 323A-1 engines.

Dornier Do 17M

A Bramo powerplant was also selected for the 13th and 14th prototypes, which received Bramo 322A-1 units and served to test the airframe and engine combination for the resulting Do 17M. This entered production as the Do 17M-1, which could carry a bombload of 1000kg (2205lb) and featured defensive armament of three trainable MG 15 rearward-firing machine guns in dorsal and ventral hatch positions, plus one firing forwards through the starboard side of the windscreen.

Once adapted for photographic reconnaissance, the Do 17M became the Do 17P, powered by two 652kW (875hp) BMW 132N engines and with a variety of different camera options. This aircraft saw production as the Do 17P-1. Further engine options were trialled in a pair of Do 17R testbeds, fitted with the 708kW (950hp) Daimler-Benz DB 600G or the 746kW (1000hp) Daimler-Benz DB 601S.

High-speed reconnaissance version

For high-speed reconnaissance, Dornier produced three examples of the Do 17S-0, which featured the DB 600G powerplant and a prone gunner's position in the underside of the forward fuselage fitted with an aft-firing MG 15 machine gun and extensive nose glazing. The variant did not progress beyond the trials phase; however, the basic design was utilized

Dornier Do 17P-1

This aircraft was flown by 3.(Fern)/Aufklarungsgruppe Nacht, a long-range night reconnaissance unit serving on the Eastern Front in December 1942.

Dornier Do 17M-1

Operated by 6./Kampfgeschwader 2, this Do 17M-1 was involved in the campaign in Poland in September 1939.

Dornier Do 17M-1
Weight (Maximum take-off) 7040kg (15,520lb)
Dimensions Length: 16.25m (53ft 3in), Wingspan: 18m (59ft), Height: 4.32m (14ft 2in)
Powerplant Two 670kW (900hp) Bramo 323A-1 radial engines
Speed 425km/h (264mph)
Range 500km (310 miles)
Ceiling 5100m (16,730ft)
Crew 4
Armament Two/three 7.92mm (0.31in) MG 15 machine guns; 1000kg (2205lb) bombload

---

Dornier Do 17P-1
Weight (Maximum take-off) 7040kg (15,520lb)
Dimensions Length: 16.25m (53ft 3in), Wingspan: 18m (59ft), Height: 4.32m (14ft 2in)
Powerplant Two 652kW (875hp) BMW 132N radial engines
Speed 425km/h (264mph)
Range 500km (310 miles)
Ceiling 5100m (16,730ft)
Crew 4
Armament Two 7.92mm (0.31in) MG 15 machine guns; provision for 1000kg (2205lb) bombload; either Rb 20/30 and Rb 50/30 or Rb 20/18 and Rb 50/18 cameras

BOMBERS

in the production-optimized Do 17U series, which resulted in a batch of 15 Do 17U-0 and Do 17U-1 aircraft. They featured a five-man crew that included two radio operators.

Dornier Do 17Z

The most prolific version of the Dornier design was the Do 17Z, of which around 1700 examples were completed between 1939 and 1940. The initial Do 17Z-0 was essentially similar to the Do 17S and was powered by two Bramo 323A-1 engines developing 671kW (900hp) each. Defensive armament consisted of three MG 15s, although the Do 17Z-1 added a fourth weapon in the nose. However, in this form the aircraft proved underpowered and its bombload was limited to 500kg (1102lb). This shortcoming was addressed in the Do 17Z-2 that followed, with 746kW (1000hp) Bramo 323P engines replacing the Bramo 323A-1s. With this change, bombload increased to 1000kg (2205lb) and up to eight defensive MG 15s could be carried.

Dornier Do 17Z-2

1./Kampfgeschwader 2 'Holzhammer' was the operating unit for this Do 17Z-2, based at Tatoi in Greece in May 1941 during Operation 'Marita', the German invasion of Greece.

A total of 22 aircraft were completed as Do 17Z-3 reconnaissance versions, while the Do 17Z-4 designation covered a dual-control trainer derivative. The Do 17Z-5 was otherwise similar to the Do 17Z-2, but was equipped with flotation bags in the fuselage and the rear of the engine nacelles for overwater operations.

Dornier Do 215

Originally developed like the Do 17K for export customers, the Do 215 was based on the Do 17Z and was initially ordered by Sweden in the shape of the Do 215A-1, which was powered by a

Dornier Do 17Z-2

Armed with 20mm (0.8in) MG/FF cannon in the nose, Do 17Z-2 R4+ZK was operated by Nachtjagdgeschwader 2 on night interdiction duties from Gilze-Rijen in the Netherlands in 1940.

Dornier Do 17Z-2

Weight (Maximum take-off) 8837kg (19,482lb)
Dimensions Length: 15.8m (51ft 10in), Wingspan: 18m (59ft 1in), Height: 4.56m (15ft)
Powerplant Two 746kW (1000hp) Bramo 323P radial engines
Speed 410km/h (255mph)
Range 660km (410 miles)
Ceiling 8200m (26,900ft)
Crew 4
Armament Six 7.92mm (0.31in) MG 15 machine guns; 1000kg (2205lb) bombload

BOMBERS

pair of 802kW (1075hp) Daimler-Benz DB 601A inverted-V engines driving three-bladed propellers.

In the event, the 18 aircraft intended for Sweden were embargoed by Germany during the production phase and redirected to the Luftwaffe, which introduced them to service as the Do 215B-0 (pre-production aircraft) and Do 215B-1 (production aircraft) – both were outfitted for long-range reconnaissance and entered service with the 3. Aufklärungsstaffel of the Oberbefehlshaber der Luftwaffe (Luftwaffe High Command) in January 1940.

There was also a pair of Do 215B-3 aircraft delivered to the Soviet Union in 1940, while the Do 215B-4 was equipped for bomber-reconnaissance duties and entered Luftwaffe service in March 1940.

As well as cameras, the Do 215B-4 featured a pair of weapon bays for a maximum of two 250kg (551lb) SC 250 bombs or 10 50kg (110lb) SC 50 bombs for short-range missions, the payload being halved for medium-

Dornier Do 215B-1
Do 215B-1 T5+AL was active on the Polish/Soviet border as of spring 1941. It was on strength with 3./Aufklärungsgruppe Oberbehlshaber der Luftwaffe (Kommando Rowehl) and used for clandestine reconnaissance of Soviet defences.

range missions; long-range sorties were flown unarmed.

The last of the Do 17 bomber and reconnaissance versions survived in frontline Luftwaffe service into the closing stages of 1942. Meanwhile, production of the Do 215B-1 and B-4 for the Luftwaffe extended into early 1941 and yielded 72 out of a planned 92 aircraft that served almost exclusively with reconnaissance formations. The last were retired from Luftwaffe service from autumn 1941, but some were transferred to the Hungarian air force, with which they remained in use into late 1942.

Dornier Do 215B-4
Another aircraft from 3./Aufklärungsgruppe Ob.d.L., this Do 215B-4 was operational in Ukraine in August 1941.

Dornier Do 215B-1
Weight (Maximum take-off) 6800kg (14,991lb)
Dimensions Length: 15.8m (51ft 10in), Wingspan: 18m (59ft 1in), Height: 4.56m (15ft)
Powerplant Two 802kW (1075hp) Daimler-Benz DB 601A inverted-V engines
Speed 470km/h (290mph)
Range 380km (240 miles)
Ceiling 9000m (30,000ft)
Crew 4
Armament Four 7.92mm (0.31in) MG 15 machine guns; 1000kg (2200lb) bombs carried internally

Dornier Do 215B-4
Weight (Maximum take-off) 6800kg (14,991lb)
Dimensions Length: 15.8m (51ft 10in), Wingspan: 18m (59ft 1in), Height: 4.56m (15ft)
Powerplant Two 802kW (1075hp) Daimler-Benz DB 601A inverted-V engines
Speed 470km/h (290mph)
Range 380km (240 miles)
Ceiling 9000m (30,000ft)
Crew 4
Armament Four 7.92mm (0.31in) MG 15 machine guns; two 250kg (551lb) SC 250 bombs or 10 50kg (110lb) SC 50 bombs; Rb 20/30 and Rb 50/30 cameras

BOMBERS

Dornier Do 217

To all intents and purposes an enlarged and further refined Do 17, the Do 215 took to the air in prototype form in August 1938.

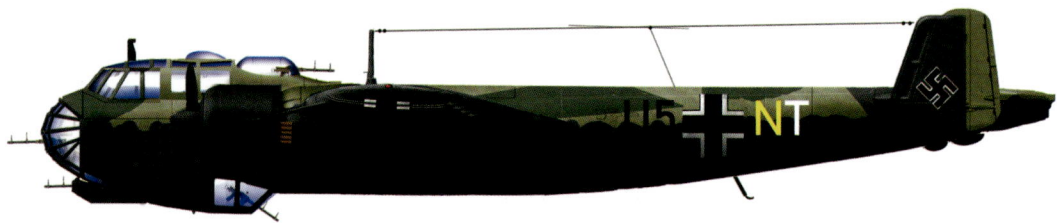

This Do 217 V1 was powered by a pair of 802kW (1075hp) Daimler-Benz DB 601A engines of the same type that had powered the export-optimized Do 215. Despite the loss of the first prototype in an accident, development continued and there were another three prototypes completed with an alternative powerplant of 708kW (960hp) Junkers Jumo 211A engines.

The last of the four prototypes, the Do 217 V4, was fitted with armament and incorporated other refinements, including enlarged vertical tail surfaces for improved stability. It was also fitted with dive brakes – the tail cone was divided into four segments that opened out when required. Another three development aircraft were produced with Jumo engines, followed by two machines that received 1156kW (1550hp) BMW 139 radial engines in an effort to improve performance. Ultimately, the improved BMW 801 was adopted for the production Do 217A version once the new engine became available in late 1939.

A reconnaissance aircraft, the Do 217A-0, entered service with the Aufklärungsgruppe Oberbefehlshaber der Luftwaffe in 1940. The eight Do 217A-0s remained pre-production aircraft, each carrying two cameras and armed with three 7.92mm (0.31in) MG 15 machine guns.

A total of five Do 217Cs were completed as the initial bomber version, the first of which (Do 217C V1) was equipped with Jumo 211A engines, while the remainder (Do 217C-0) utilized BD 601A engines. All of the C-models were armed with five MG 15s and could carry a bombload of 3000kg (6614lb), a major advance over the 1000kg (2205lb) carried by the Do 17Z.

Dornier Do 217E

While the A- and C-series were destined to be produced in strictly limited numbers, the first major production version was the Do 217E that appeared in 1940. This model was characterized by a deepened fuselage accommodating an enlarged bomb bay for the carriage of larger bombs or a torpedo.

Dornier Do 217E-4

U5+NT was flown by 9./Kampfgeschwader 2 'Holzhammer' based at Gilze-Rijen in the Netherlands in 1942. It was involved in countering the Allied Dieppe raid in August that year.

Dornier Do 217E-4
Weight (Maximum take-off) 15,290kg (33,700lb)
Dimensions Length: 17.25m (56ft 6in), Wingspan: 19m (62ft 4in), Height: 4.8m (15ft 8in)
Powerplant Two 1147kW (1539hp) BMW 801A air-cooled 14-cylinder radial aircraft engines
Speed 535km/h (332mph)
Range 2400km (1490 miles)
Ceiling 8200m (26,900ft)
Crew 4
Armament One 13mm (0.51in) MG 131 (dorsal turret), three 7.92mm (0.31in) MG 15 machine guns (forward fuselage), two 15mm (0.59in) MG 151/15 cannon (nose and ventral position); 3000kg (6614lb) bombload

Despite these changes, the Do 217E first became operational in the reconnaissance role, joining 3.(F)/11 towards the end of 1940. In its bomber guise, it first saw service with II./KG 40 in spring 1941.

Subvariants of the Do 217E included the Do 217E-1 that could carry a 3000kg (6614lb) bombload and featured bolstered defensive armament compared to the Do 217C – a 15mm (0.59in) MG 151/15 cannon in the nose as well as the five MG 15s of the previous bomber version.

Even heavier firepower was offered by the Do 217E-2, which featured a 13mm (0.51in) MG 131 machine gun in a dorsal turret, a second MG 151 in a ventral position, three MG 15s in the forward fuselage and the MG 151/15 cannon in the nose. A further development for the maritime strike mission was the Do 217E-3. Optimized for anti-shipping operations over the Atlantic, the E-3 was fitted with extra armour protection for the crew plus additional internal tanks for a further 750 litres (165 Imp gal) of fuel. This subvariant carried a single 20mm (0.8in) MG FF cannon in the nose as well as seven MG 15 machine guns.

In 1941 the Do 217E-4 began to roll off the production line, this being an updated E-2 with BMW 801C engines and cable-cutters in the leading edges of the wings to defeat barrage balloons. There was also a batch of 65 Do 217E-5 aircraft completed for carriage of the Henschel Hs 293 guided missile, two of which could be carried on underwing racks. The 21st Do 217E was experimentally equipped with turbocharged DB 601 engines, but it was only used for trial purposes.

The Do 217E was the first bomber version; its later subvariants could launch Henschel Hs 293 guided bombs.

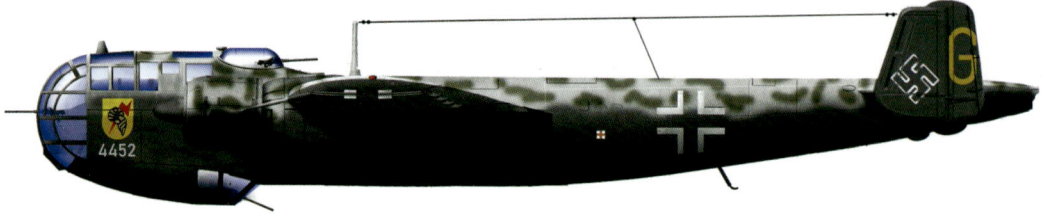

Dornier Do 217K-1
Do 217K-1 4452 'Yellow G' wears the unit markings of 3./Kampfgeschwader 2, based in France during 1943–44.

Dornier Do 217K

In autumn 1942 the next major version appeared in the form of the Do 217K. The initial-production Do 217K-1 introduced a new glazed nose and an unstepped cockpit. A further bomber variant was the Do 217K-2 that had provision for two SD 1400X (Fritz-X) guided bombs below the wing and with the associated FuG 203a and FuG 230a guidance equipment in the fuselage. An example of this variant was responsible for sinking the Italian battleship *Roma* on 14 September 1943, when aircraft from the Marseilles-based III./KG 100

Dornier Do 217M-1
Another Kampfgeschwader 2 aircraft, this example was assigned to the 9. Staffel (9./KG 2) and stationed in France in 1944.

Dornier Do 217K-1
Weight (Maximum take-off) 12,700kg (28,000lb)
Dimensions Length: 17.12m (56ft 2in), Wingspan: 19m (62ft 4in), Height: 4.8m (15ft 8in)
Powerplant Two 1073kW (1440hp) BMW 801L engines
Speed 520km/h (323mph)
Range 2150km (1335 miles)
Ceiling 7350m (24,114ft)
Crew 4
Armament Twin-barreled 7.92mm (0.31in) MG 81Z machine gun in the nose, two 7.92mm (0.31in) MG 81s (beam positions), two 7.92mm (0.31in) MG 131s (dorsal turret and ventral position); 2500kg (5511lb) internal bombload

intercepted the warship as the Italian fleet attempted to break out of La Spezia to join the Allies.

The Do 217K-3 was another missile-carrier, with provision for either the Hs 293 or the unpowered SD 1400X. Development of the K-series continued and yielded the Do 217L, two experimental aircraft being completed with a modified cockpit and revised defensive positions.

The Do 217M, meanwhile, was broadly similar to the Do 217K. The Do 217M-1 was equivalent to the Do 217K-1 but was powered by two DB 603A engines; the Do 217K-5 was similar to the K-1 but had an under-fuselage rack to accommodate an Hs 293 missile. The M-series equivalent to the Do 217K-3 was

Dornier Do 217M-1
Weight (Maximum take-off) 16,790kg (37,015lb)
Dimensions Length: 17.25m (56ft 6in), Wingspan: 19m (62ft 4in), Height: 4.8m (15ft 8in)
Powerplant Two 1162kW (1558hp) Daimler-Benz DB 603A-1 V12 engines
Speed 520km/h (323mph)
Range 2150km (1335 miles)
Ceiling 7350m (24,114ft)
Crew 4
Armament Twin-barreled 7.92mm (0.31in) MG 81Z machine gun in the nose, two 7.92mm (0.31in) MG 81s (beam positions), two 7.92mm (0.31in) MG 131s (dorsal turret and ventral position); 2500kg (5511lb) internal bombload

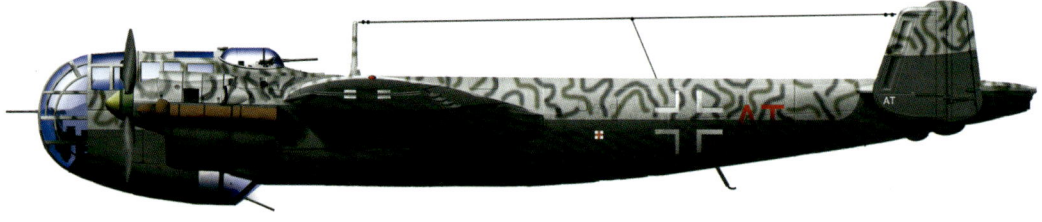

BOMBERS

the Do 217M-3, again with the DB 603A engines, while the Do 217M-11 featured extended-span wings and was also a missile-carrier.

Dornier Do 217P

Last of the bomber/reconnaissance line was the Do 217P, first flown in prototype form in June 1942. The P-series was developed as a high-altitude reconnaissance platform and featured a pressurized cabin and powerplant of two 1305kW (1750hp) DB 603B engines. These were provided with a two-stage supercharger that was in turn driven by a 1100kW (1475hp) DB 605T engine fitted in the bomb bay.

Armament consisted of four 7.92mm (0.31in) MG 81 machine guns, and the three Do 217P-0 pre-production aircraft were each equipped with three cameras.

A total of around 1730 Do 217s of all types was eventually completed.

Dornier Do 317

Mention should also be made of the Do 317, intended as an advanced medium bomber to succeed the He 111 and Ju 88. It was based on the layout of the Do 217, with provision for a four-man crew in a pressurized cabin.

Although rejected for the bomber requirement, five examples were completed under the Do 217R designation. These featured DB 603 engines and provision for a pair of Hs 293 missiles but lacked pressurization. These unique aircraft served with III./KG 100 based at Orléans in France.

Dornier Do 217M-11

Utilized for test and evaluation and captured at Flensburg in April 1945, this Do 217M-11 was equipped with the revised tail fins and rudders of the Do 317.

Dornier Do 217M-11

Weight (Maximum take-off) 16,790kg (37,015lb)
Dimensions Length: 17.25m (56ft 6in), Wingspan: 19m (62ft 4in), Height: 4.8m (15ft 8in)
Powerplant Two 1162kW (1558hp) Daimler-Benz DB 603A-1 V12 engines
Speed 520km/h (323mph)
Range 2150km (1335 miles)
Ceiling 7350m (24,114ft)
Crew 4
Armament Twin-barreled 7.92mm (0.31in) MG 81Z machine gun in the nose, two 7.92mm (0.31in) MG 81s (beam positions), two 7.92mm (0.31in) MG 131s (dorsal turret and ventral position); provision for one Fritz-X/Hs-293 anti-ship glide bomb under fuselage

---

This Do 217E-4 served with II./KG 40, the first unit to use Do 217s in action. They were employed in anti-shipping roles against the British. Note the lateral-firing MG 15 in the aft portion of the flight deck.

27

BOMBERS

Junkers Ju 88

Remembered as the Luftwaffe's most versatile warplane in World War II, the Ju 88 was produced in successively improved variants until the end of the conflict.

The Junkers Ju 88 began life as a project to meet a 1935 *Reichsluftfahrtministerium* (German Air Ministry) requirement for a three-seat high-speed bomber (*Schnellbomber*) able to fly at 500km/h (311mph) while carrying a bombload of 800kg (1765lb). The rival Henschel Hs 127 and Messerschmitt Bf 162 were also offered. The initial Ju 88 prototype, with the civilian registration D-AQEN, powered by a pair of 746kW (1000hp) Daimler-Benz DB 600Aa 12-cylinder engines in annular cowlings, completed a maiden flight on 21 December 1936.

The first prototype was lost in a crash in early 1937, being replaced by the second, D-AREN, first flown on 10 April that year. The third prototype, D-ASAZ, introduced Junkers Jumo 211A engines of the same rating as the first two aircraft and achieved a speed of 520km/h (323mph) during evaluation. Other changes included a raised canopy line for installation of a rear-firing 7.92mm (0.31in) MG 15 machine gun, a more rounded rudder of increased area and a bombsight in a blister below the nose. Encouraged by this early performance potential, the fifth prototype was used in a successful bid to claim the 1000km (621 mile) closed-circuit record with a speed of 517km/h (321mph) carrying a 2000kg (4409lb) payload.

The production Ju 88 would differ from the initial prototypes in adding a fourth crewmember, increased armament and dive-bombing capability. The first two features had been trialled in the fourth prototype, V4, flown in February 1938, which also incorporated the 'beetle eye' crew compartment with ventral bomb-aiming cupolas armed with a rear-firing MG 15. The Ju 88 V5 (D-ATYU) was similar to the fourth but with 895kW (1200hp) Jumo 211B-1 engines, while the V6 (D-ASCY) was considered the first pre-production aircraft for the Ju 88A, with four-bladed propellers, Jumo 211B-1s and a redesigned main undercarriage and engine nacelle arrangement. After the similar V7, the V8 and V9 introduced slatted dive brakes for a dive-bombing

A trio of Ju 88A-4s from III./LG 1 is seen over the Mediterranean Sea in 1942. The aircraft have the bulged rear canopy glazing, which allowed easy firing of the twin MG 81 defensive guns.

BOMBERS

Junkers Ju 88A-4
Wearing the codes 5K+NK, this Ju 88A-4 was assigned to 2./Kampfgeschwader 3, fighting on the Eastern Front in the winter of 1942/43.

Junkers Ju 88A-4
Ship-killing Ju 88A-4 A6+HH was the aircraft of Major Werner Baumbach, flying with 1./Kampfgeschwader 30 based in Norway in 1941. Note the personal tally on the tail fin.

Junkers Ju 88A-4

Weight (Maximum take-off) 14,000kg (30,860lb)
Dimensions Length: 14.4m (47ft 3in), Wingspan: 20m (65ft 7.5in), Height: 4.8m (15ft 8in)
Powerplant Two 1051kW (1410hp) Junkers Jumo 211J-2 engines
Speed 470km/h (292mph)
Range 2700km (1677 miles)
Ceiling 8200m (26,900ft)
Crew 4
Armament Four 7.92mm (0.31in) MG 81J machine guns, one 7.92mm (0.31in) MG 81Z twin machine gun; up to 1400kg (3100lb) bomload

capability. The final prototype, V10, tested external bomb racks between the fuselage and engine nacelles.

After the 10 prototypes, the first of 10 pre-production Ju 88A-0 bombers took to the air in early 1939, serving in an experimental basis with Erprobungskommando 88 from March 1939, and was followed by the Ju 88A-1 production version that entered service in September that year with I./KG 30. The production effort was mammoth, with Arado, Dornier, Heinkel, Henschel and Volkswagen all being involved, as well as two Junkers factories in Schönebeck and Aschersleben.

The Ju 88 was available for operational service during the invasion of Poland, in which I./KG 30 flew its first mission with the type on 26 September 1939; both pre-production Ju 88A-0 and Ju 88A-1 production aircraft were involved. These switched

KAMPFGESCHWADER 30

Established at Greifswald in November 1939, Kampfgeschwader 30 (KG 30) consisted of three *Gruppen* by January 1940, before moving to Barth and adding a fourth *Gruppe* in April 1941. Flying the Ju 88 from the outset, KG 30 was a dedicated anti-shipping unit: it first saw action in the role in October 1939 attacking warships off Rosyth, Scotland. II./KG 30 took part in the invasion of Norway before moving to Chièvres, Belgium, in June 1940. In September 1942, KG 30 was active in the devastating attack on Arctic convoy PQ 18, but by November 1944 had been re-designated as a fighter unit.

BOMBERS

Junkers Ju 88A-5
Based at Westerland-Sylt, the I. Gruppe of Kampfgeschwader 30 was the first to use the Ju 88 in combat, its initial mission involving an anti-shipping attack on British warships in the Firth of Forth on 26 September 1939.

Crew
The Ju 88 was usually operated by a crew of four, comprising a pilot, co-pilot/bomb aimer, radio operator/ventral gunner and a flight engineer/rear gunner.

Defensive Armament
The pilot had acess to a forward-firing MG 15 machine gun that was arranged to fire through the starboard windscreen. One or two similar weapons were usually fitted at the rear of the cockpit.

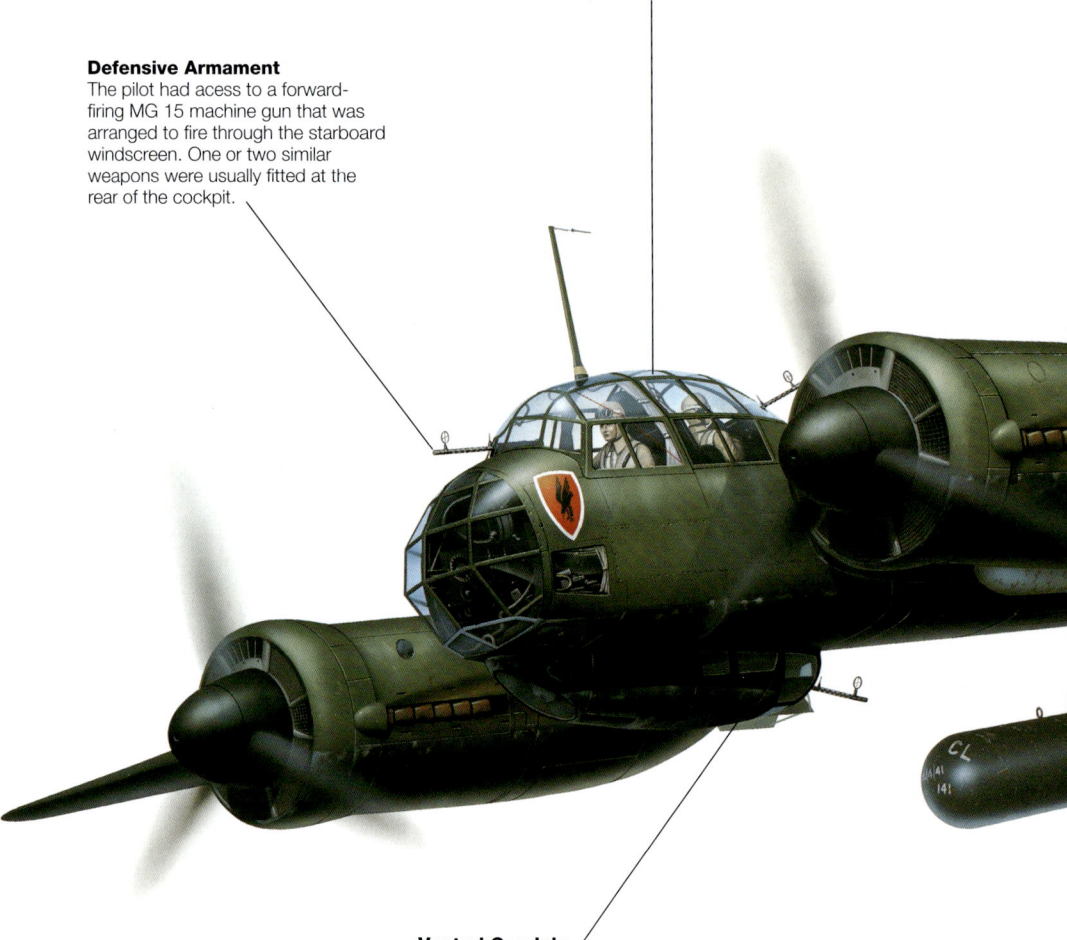

Ventral Gondola
As well as being armed with a fourth defensive MG 15, this was used by the bomb aimer.

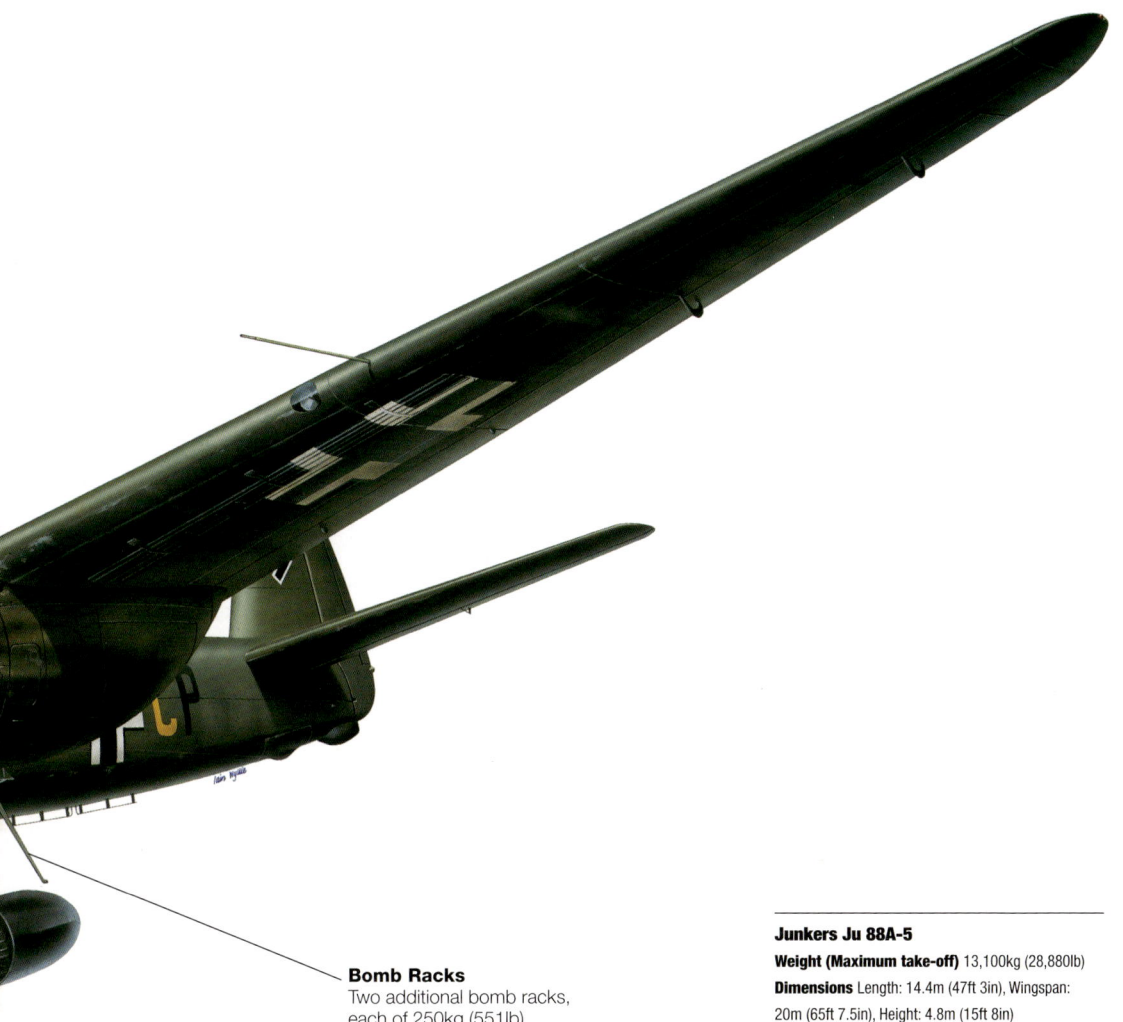

Bomb Racks
Two additional bomb racks, each of 250kg (551lb) capacity, could be fitted below the outer wing panels.

Junkers Ju 88A-5
Weight (Maximum take-off) 13,100kg (28,880lb)
Dimensions Length: 14.4m (47ft 3in), Wingspan: 20m (65ft 7.5in), Height: 4.8m (15ft 8in)
Powerplant Two 1051kW (1200hp) Junkers Jumo 213B-1 liquid-cooled piston engines
Speed 470km/h (292mph)
Range 2700km (1677 miles)
Ceiling 8200m (26,900ft)
Crew 4
Armament Four 7.92mm (0.31in) MG 15 machine guns (windscreen, nose, rear cockpit, ventral), two upward-firing 20mm MG 151/20 cannon (mid-plane); 1500–2000kg (3310–4410lb) bombload

BOMBERS

back to three-bladed propellers, which were retained throughout the subsequent bomber versions.

Lessons of the type's early combat missions led to the addition of further defensive armament; the ventral position was revised to accommodate two MG 15s and additional weapons were arranged to fire laterally from the sides of the cockpit (the pilot was already provided with a single MG 15 in the starboard side of the windscreen).

More comprehensive changes came with the Ju 88A-4 version that featured an increased wingspan and structural strengthening in order to carry greater loads – including enhanced defensive armament with 7.92mm (0.31in) MG 81s replacing the previous MG 15s. The powerplant was also to be upgraded

Junkers Ju 88A-5
Ju 88A-5 L1+GN was operated by 5./Lehrgeschwader 1, which was based in Italy as of April 1941 to take part in the Greek campaign.

to the Jumo 211F or 211J, while the ailerons were changed from fabric to metal, and the undercarriage was beefed up. With the new Jumo 211F or 211J engine still not ready, production of the new version commenced with the A-1's engines, creating the interim Ju 88A-5 that saw widespread use in the Battle of Britain.

A- and B-series
Ultimately, the A-series extended to include subvariants up to the Ju 88A-17. In the process, key subvariants included the Ju 88A-2 with Jumo 211G-1 engines (with similar rating to the Jumo 211B-1) and provision for rocket-assisted take-off (RATO) gear; Ju 88A-3 and A-7 dual-control trainers; Ju 88A-6 anti-balloon aircraft; and the tropicalized Ju 88A-9 and A-10.

The Ju 88B was developed while production of the Ju 88A was underway and featured a more extensively glazed nose and a revised powerplant of two

Junkers Ju 88A-5
This aircraft was flown by *Unteroffizier* Peter Stahl during the Night Blitz over the UK in 1940. The operating unit was the 9. Staffel of II./Kampfgeschwader 30. The A-5 version utilized a long-span wing developed for the delayed A-4 bomber.

Junkers Ju 88A-5
Weight (Maximum take-off) 13,100kg (28,880lb)
Dimensions Length: 14.4m (47ft 3in), Wingspan: 20m (65ft 7.5in), Height: 4.8m (15ft 8in)
Powerplant Two 1051kW (1200hp) Junkers Jumo 213B-1 liquid-cooled piston engines
Speed 470km/h (292mph)
Range 2700km (1677 miles)
Ceiling 8200m (26,900ft)
Crew 4
Armament Four 7.92mm (0.31in) MG 15 machine guns (windscreen, nose, rear cockpit, ventral), two upward-firing 20mm (0.8in) MG 151/20 cannon (mid-plane); 1500–2000kg (3310–4410lb) bombload

---

BOMBERS

LEHRGESCHWADER 1

Formally a training wing, Lehrgeschwader 1 (LG 1) was in practice a multi-role unit responsible for a variety of fighter, bomber and dive-bomber *Gruppen*. The unit's Ju 88s went into battle during the campaigns in France and the Low Countries in 1940 and then took part in the Battle of Britain. During the campaigns in the Balkans and North Africa LG 1 took part in anti-shipping operations, before returning to France to support the beleaguered German Army during the Normandy Campaign and the Battle of the Bulge.

Junkers Ju 88A-14

Ju 88A-14 L1+EA was also operated by Lehrgeschwader 1. It was assigned to the *Geschwader Stab* and based at Catania, Sicily, in 1941.

1193kW (1600hp) BMW 801MA radial engines. However, this resulted in only a minor improvement in performance and just 10 pre-production Ju 88B-0 aircraft were built.

D-series

While the Ju 88C was a heavy fighter and night fighter series, the D-series comprised long-range reconnaissance

Junkers Ju 88A-14

Weight (Maximum take-off) 14,000kg (30,860lb)
Dimensions Length: 14.4m (47ft 3in), Wingspan: 20m (65ft 7.5in), Height: 4.8m (15ft 8in)
Powerplant Two 1051kW (1410hp) Junkers Jumo 211J-2 engines
Speed 470km/h (292mph)
Range 2700km (1677 miles)
Ceiling 8200m (26,900ft)
Crew 4
Armament Armament Four 7.92mm (0.31in) MG 81J machine guns (windscreen, rear cockpit, rear ventral), one 20mm (0.8in) MG FF cannon (ventral gondola); up to 1400kg (3100lb) bombload

Junkers Ju 88A-11

Another Lehrgeschwader 1 aircraft, Ju 88A-11 L1+LW was on strength with the wing's 12. Staffel fighting in North Africa in 1942.

Junkers Ju 88A-11

Weight (Maximum take-off) 14,000kg (30,860lb)
Dimensions Length: 14.4m (47ft 3in), Wingspan: 20m (65ft 7.5in), Height: 4.8m (15ft 8in)
Powerplant Two 1051kW (1410hp) Junkers Jumo 211J-2 engines
Speed 470km/h (292mph)
Range 2700km (1677 miles)
Ceiling 8200m (26,900ft)
Crew 4
Armament Four 7.92mm (0.31in) MG 81J machine guns, one 7.92mm (0.31in) MG 81Z twin machine gun; up to 1400kg (3100lb) bombload

aircraft that were based on the airframe of the Ju 88A-4 and which entered service in summer 1940. Production subvariants were the Ju 88D-1 to Ju 88D-5, with detail differences in terms of engines and equipment. The

BOMBERS

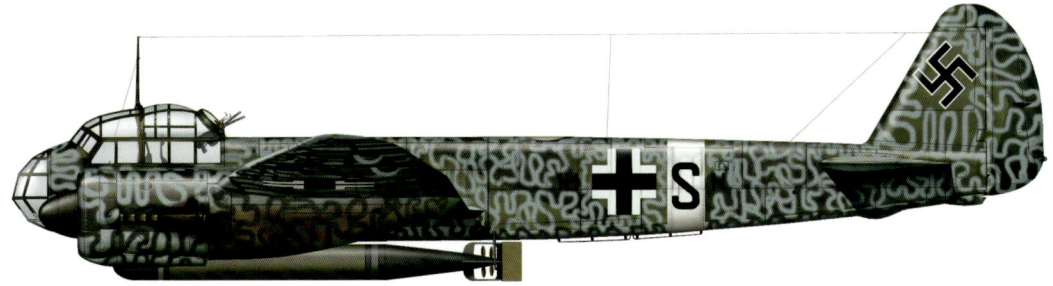

D-series, like the Ju 88A-4, had been intended to use the Jumo 211F or 211J engine from the outset, but these were initially unavailable, so early Ju 88Ds were therefore equivalent to the interim Ju 88A-5. The reconnaissance aircraft retained the four-man crew but featured a reduced defensive armament of just three MG 15s. The D-series was also exported to Hungary and Romania.

The Ju 88G was another series of night fighters, while the Ju 88H featured a lengthened fuselage for additional internal fuel capacity; this was produced as the Ju 88H-1 reconnaissance aircraft and the Ju 88H-2 fighter.

Anti-armour Junkers
Another further development of the Ju 88A-4 was the Ju 88P. It was intended for close support, including anti-armour operations, and was built as the Ju 88P-1 from summer 1942 with a single 75mm (2.96in) PaK 40 or BK 7,5 cannon and a solid nose. There was also the subsequent Ju 88P-2 to P-4 that featured different combinations of heavy anti-tank weaponry. The P-2 subvariant was armed with a pair of 37mm (1.45in) BK 3,7 cannon, which was judged more effective than the heavier, slow-firing 75mm weapons, while the P-4 introduced a low-drag fairing containing a single 50mm (1.96in) BK 5 cannon.

The Ju 88H-1 was another reconnaissance variant, produced by combining the wings and BMW 801 radial engines of the Ju 88G-1 fighter

Junkers Ju 88A-17
Torpedo-armed Ju 88A-17 1H+SH was flown by Kampfgeschwader 26. The aircraft was based in Bardufoss, Norway, in early 1945.

Junkers Ju 88D-1
Wearing an unusual silver-doped finish, Ju 88D-1 4U+GK carries underwing fuel tanks for its long-range reconnaissance role with 2.(Fern)/Aufklärungsgruppe 123. This aircraft crashed in Italy in February 1941.

Junkers Ju 88A-17
Weight (Maximum take-off) 14,000kg (30,860lb)
Dimensions Length: 14.4m (47ft 3in), Wingspan: 20m (65ft 7.5in), Height: 4.8m (15ft 8in)
Powerplant Two 1051kW (1410hp) Junkers Jumo 211J-2 engines
Speed 470km/h (292mph)
Range 2700km (1677 miles)
Ceiling 8200m (26,900ft)
Crew 3
Armament Two 7.92mm (0.31in) MG 15 machine guns (rear cockpit); one PVC torpedo rack under each wing

Junkers Ju 88D-1
Weight (Maximum take-off) 11,300kg (24,900lb)
Dimensions Length: 14.36m (47ft 1in), Wingspan: 20m (65ft 7.5in), Height: 5.07m (16ft 7in)
Powerplant Two 1051kW (1410hp) Junkers Jumo 211J-2 engines
Speed 475km/h (295mph)
Range 3100km (1920 miles)
Ceiling 8600m (28,200ft)
Crew 4
Armament Three 7.92mm (0.31in) MG 15 machine guns (windscreen, rear cockpit)

BOMBERS

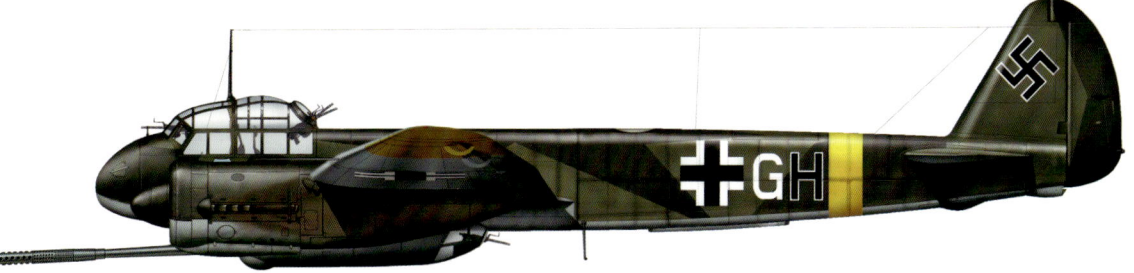

with the camera-equipped airframe of the Ju 88D-1. The fuselage was stretched fore and aft of the wing, providing space for additional internal fuel for a range of 5150km (3200 miles). In total, 10 examples were completed for operations over the Atlantic.

High-altitude pathfinder

In an effort to wring out more performance from the basic design to provide a better chance of evading Allied fighters, Junkers developed the Ju 88S high-altitude pathfinder/bomber and Ju 88T reconnaissance aircraft that became the final major production versions. The Ju 88S, first flown in late 1942, was characterized by its curved glazed nosecone and BMW 801 radials. The initial series-production machine was the Ju 88S-1 with BMW 801G engines featuring nitrous oxide boost, while the Ju 88S-2 featured turbo-supercharged BMW 801TJ engines and a wooden ventral pannier replacing the bomb bays and racks. Gun armament

Junkers Ju 88P-1

The *Versuchskommando fur Panzerbekampfung* (Anti-tank Test Command) employed this Ju-88P-1 for trials work. The unit was formed at Rechlin in July 1942 and sent elements to the Eastern Front for combat trials.

of the S-series was reduced to just a single 13mm (0.51in) MG 131 machine gun, and the variant was flown by a three-man crew.

The T-series, meanwhile, entered production in spring 1944, replacing the Ju 88D and remaining in use in small numbers until the end of the war.

By the time production came to an end, almost 15,000 examples of the Ju 88 series had been produced.

Junkers Ju 88S-3

1./Kampfgeschwader 66 flew this Ju 88S-3. This aircraft slid off the runway at Rhein-Main near Frankfurt in winter 1944. The 'squiggle' camouflage scheme was intended to provide protection for the aircraft parked on the ground and in the open.

Junkers Ju 88P-1
Weight (Maximum take-off) 14,000kg (30,860lb)
Dimensions Length: 14.4m (47ft 3in), Wingspan: 20m (65ft 7.5in), Height: 4.8m (15ft 8in)
Powerplant Two 1051kW (1410hp) Junkers Jumo 211J-2 engines
Speed 470km/h (292mph)
Range 2700km (1677 miles)
Ceiling 7000m (22,960ft)
Crew 4
Armament One 75mm (2.96in) BK 7,5 cannon, four 7.92mm (0.31in) MG 15 machine guns (windscreen, rear cockpit, ventral)

Junkers Ju 88S-3
Weight (Maximum take-off) 14,000kg (30,860lb)
Dimensions Length: 14.4m (47ft 3in), Wingspan: 20m (65ft 7.5in), Height: 4.8m (15ft 8in)
Powerplant Two 1671kW (2240hp) Jumo 213A engines and GM-1 boost system
Speed 614km/h (382mph)
Range 2700km (1677 miles)
Ceiling 8500m (27,900ft)
Crew 3
Armament One 13mm (0.51in) MG 131 machine gun (rear cockpit)

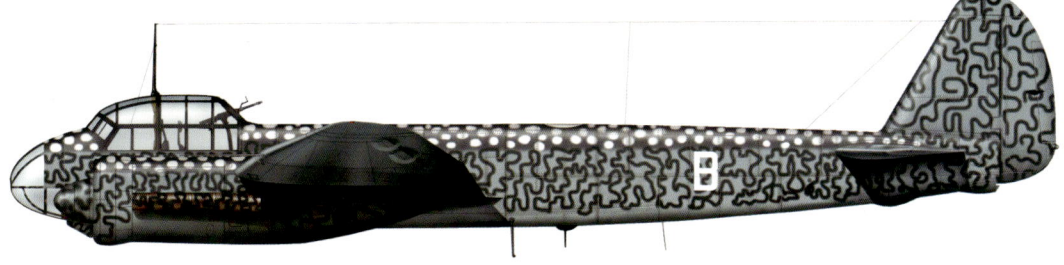

BOMBERS

Junkers Ju 88 *Mistel* bombers

A proposal for the *Mistel* ('mistletoe') composite aircraft was first made in 1943 with the aim of using time-expired Ju 88 airframes adapted as pilotless missiles.

These would be flown to the target by an attached Messerschmitt Bf 109 or Focke-Wulf Fw 190 fighter flying 'piggyback' atop the bomber. The pilot of the fighter would aim the Ju 88 at the target before commanding its release and then departing for base.

Early trials in 1942 made use of a lightweight Klemm sports plane mounted on the back of a DFS 230A glider, with the resulting combination being towed aloft by a Junkers Ju 52/3m transport. In subsequent trials, the Klemm was replaced by heavier aircraft, first a Focke-Wulf Stosser and later the intended Bf 109.

A prototype bomber/fighter combination was first flown in July 1943 and proved to be generally practical. The major drawback was that the Ju 88 'missile' became unguided as soon as it was released by the fighter and relied upon its on-board autopilot to maintain steady flight as it headed to its target, whereupon its warhead would detonate. At the time the war came to an end, work was underway on a guidance system that would have ensured greater accuracy. The warhead was typically an 3800kg (8380lb) hollow-charge device with a long standoff fuse, fitted in the nose of the bomber. The ideal release point was judged to be around 1000 metres (0.6 miles) from the target, but this would leave the *Mistel* at the mercy of anti-aircraft fire.

Main composites

Several different composites were completed, including the *Mistel* 1 that was used operationally, and which combined the Ju 88A-4 with a Bf 109F; it was also available in a training version as the *Mistel* S-1. The *Mistel* 2 (and S-2) combined the Ju 88G-1 with an Fw 190A-8 or Fw 190F-8/U3; while the *Mistel* 3a (and S-3a) were produced by combining the Ju 88A-6 with an Fw 190A-6.

Indeed, by 1945, Ju 88G-10 and Ju 88H-4 aircraft were being produced in the factory for dedicated *Mistel* work and were never flown as ordinary

Mistel 1: Ju 88A-4/Bf 109F-2

This *Mistel* 1 combination comprised a Ju 88A-4 with a Bf 109F-2. It was operated by IV./Kampfgeschwader 101.

Mistel 1
Weight (loaded) 33,780kg (74,472lb)
Dimensions Length: 14.36m (47ft 1in), Wingspan: 20.08m (65ft 9in), Height: 13.97m (45ft 9in)
Powerplant One 993kW (1332hp) DB 601E radial piston engine, two 1051kW (1410hp) Jumo 211 J-1 radial piston engines
Speed 380km/h (236mph)
Range 1650km (1025 miles)
Ceiling 10,655m (34,950ft)
Crew 1
Armament 3800kg (8380lb) hollow-charge device

BOMBERS

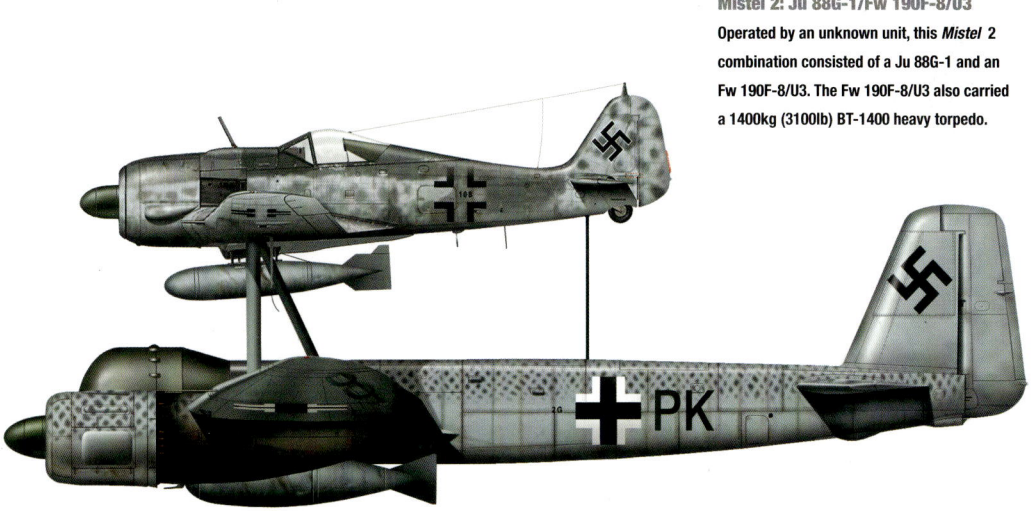

Mistel 2: Ju 88G-1/Fw 190F-8/U3
Operated by an unknown unit, this *Mistel* 2 combination consisted of a Ju 88G-1 and an Fw 190F-8/U3. The Fw 190F-8/U3 also carried a 1400kg (3100lb) BT-1400 heavy torpedo.

Mistel 2: Ju 88G-1/Fw 190F-8
Another *Mistel* 2 assigned to an unidentified unit, this also consisted of a Ju 88G-1 lower component and an Fw 190F-8.

Mistel 2
Weight (loaded) 33,780kg (74,472lb)
Dimensions Length: 14.36m (47ft 1in), Wingspan: 20.08m (65ft 9in), Height: 13.97m (45ft 9in)
Powerplant One 1500kW (2000PS) BMW 801S radial engine, two 1250kW (1677hp) BMW 801G-2 double-row radial piston engines
Speed 380km/h (236mph)
Range 1650km (1025 miles)
Ceiling 10,655m (34,950ft)
Crew 1
Armament Up to 3800kg (8380lb) hollow-charge device

BOMBERS

aircraft. The name *Vater und Sohn* ('father and son') was also applied to these composite aircraft by Luftwaffe crews.

For long-range missions, the *Mistel* 3b and 3c were produced using a combination of Ju 88G-10 or Ju 88H-4 with an Fw 190A-8 equipped with overwing auxiliary fuel tanks; the fighter used a different fuel grade and was unable to draw fuel from the lower component. Some of these composite aircraft were not intended for attacking targets, but to serve as pathfinders for larger *Mistel* formations. The lower (Ju 88) component retained a three-man crew and its accompanying Fw 190 was to be launched in an emergency, after which it would provide escort fighter cover.

Operational use

The *Mistel* was first put to operational use on 24/25 June 1944, when the composite aircraft were launched in an attack against Allied blockships that formed part of the Mulberry temporary harbour in the Baie de la Seine, France. One aircraft was forced to jettison its bomb on the way to the target, but the other four achieved some level of success; all five pilots returned safely. However, a planned raid by KG 101 against the British fleet's naval base at Scapa Flow was never launched. Other targets included major bridges that were attacked on both the Eastern and Western Fronts in the closing months of the war in Europe, including the vital Nijmegen bridge over the Waal – the latter raid failed to hit their British-held target. Another plan to attack the Royal Navy saw a *Mistel* squadron deploy to Denmark, but when the British sank the battleship *Tirpitz*, the warships that had threatened the German fleet departed the area and the *Mistels* were deprived of their targets.

Following early service with KG 101, the *Mistel* was passed on to KG 200 – tasked with special missions – within a task force named 'Helbig'. In one episode that demonstrated the risk inherent in the mission, an attack on the bridge over the Oder at Göritz saw one composite pilot forced to release his bomb early, while the other three pressed on, two scoring direct hits and one a near miss. This came at the cost of six 'flying bomb' Ju 88s and two Bf 109 control aircraft lost.

Other combinations

Among other *Mistel* combinations that were trialled before the war came to an end was a Ju 88G-7 and Focke-Wulf Ta 152H fighter. As well as Ju 88s, the lower component of the *Mistel* could also be provided by the Focke-Wulf Ta 154 two-seat night fighter. A total of six conversions were completed in which a Ta 154A-0 pre-production aircraft was fitted with a 2000kg (4409lb) warhead in the nose and supports for the Fw 190 whose pilot was to control the combination.

In total, around 250 of these composite aircraft were completed, but the lack of terminal guidance ensured that their effectiveness was limited.

Mistel 3B

Weight (loaded) 33,780kg (74,472lb)
Dimensions Length: 15.50m (50ft 9in), Wingspan: 20.08m (65ft 9in), Height: 13.97m (45ft 9in)
Powerplant One 1250kW (1677hp) BMW 801D-2 14-cylinder radial engine, two 1267kW (1700hp) BMW 801 radial piston engines
Speed 380km/h (236mph)
Range 1650km (1025 miles)
Ceiling 10,655m (34,950ft)
Crew 1
Armament Up to 3800kg (8380lb) hollow-charge device

Mistel 3B: Ju 88H-4 Fürungsmachine/ Fw 190A-8

In Mistel 3B combination, the stretched Ju 88H-4 airframe served as the *Führungsmaschine* – an ultra-long-range pathfinder – attached to an Fw 190A-8 fighter escort.

Heinkel He 177

The He 177 heavy bomber traces its origins back to the P.1041 project for a long-range bomber that emerged amid mid-1930s plans to field a strategic bombing force for the Luftwaffe.

These efforts were eventually abandoned but the idea of a heavy bomber was revisited in 1938 when the *Reichsluftfahrtministerium* (German Air Ministry) approached Heinkel with a new requirement for an aircraft in this class.

The new bomber first flew in prototype (He 177 V1) form on 19 November 1939. With no available engine in the 1492kW (2000hp) class at this time, the aircraft instead made use of a pair of close-coupled Daimler-Benz DB 606 units – effectively, two DB 601s combined in each nacelle to produce 1939kW (2600hp) and driving single propellers. Another oddity of the design was the undercarriage, consisting of twin main landing gear units on each side, which retracted sideways into the wing, inboard and outboard of each engine nacelle.

Accident-prone prototypes

The early aircraft suffered from numerous teething troubles and at least three prototypes were lost in accidents that were attributed to weaknesses of the wing structure or engine fires. While the structural shortcomings were quickly overcome, the engines' propensity to overheat was never entirely addressed. Meanwhile, development trials continued with a batch of 35 pre-production He 177A-0 aircraft, some of which were also used for conversion training.

The first of the initial-production He 177A-1 aircraft began to be delivered to I./KG 40 in July 1942 for operational trials, but still suffered from the structural problems that had afflicted their predecessors. Total production of the A-1 amounted to 130 aircraft, all of which were completed by Arado, in four discrete subvariants – He 177A-1/R1 to He 177A-1/R4, all with minor variations.

Heinkel He 177A-3

In late 1942, the more reliable He 177A-3 entered service and aircraft based in France took part in raids against targets in the UK during Operation 'Steinbock'. The 170 He 177A-3s were completed by Heinkel, the first of these being He 177A-3/R1 bombers with DB 606A/B engines, while subsequent deliveries were powered by DB 610 engines.

The He 177A-3/R2 featured improved armament, while the He 177A-3/R3 was a missile-carrier

Heinkel He 177A-3/R-2
Named 'Edith', this He 177A-3/R-2 was operated by 2./Kampfgeschwader 100 based at Châteaudun, France, in October 1944.

Heinkel He 177A-3/R-2
Weight (Maximum take-off) 32,000kg (70,548lb)
Dimensions Length: 22m (72ft 2in), Wingspan: 31.44m (103ft 2in), Height: 6.67m (21ft 11in)
Powerplant Two 2133kW (2860hp) Daimler-Benz DB 610 24-cylinder liquid-cooled piston engines
Speed 565km/h (351mph)
Range 1540km (960 miles)
Ceiling 8000m (26,000ft)
Crew 6
Armament Two 20mm (0.8in) MG 151 cannon (front ventral gondola and tail), four 13mm (0.51in) MG 131 machine guns (cockpit, rear gondola, forward dorsal turret, aft dorsal turret); Up to 7000kg (15,000lb) of ordnance internally, up to 2500kg (5,500lb) externally on underwing racks

BOMBERS

with provision to carry up to three Henschel Hs 293 weapons. Another missile-carrier, the He 177A-3/R4 was equipped with FuG 203 missile-control equipment in a gondola.

Alternative weapons were the features of the He 177A-3/R5 and He 177A-3/R7, respectively armed with a single 75mm (2.96in) cannon in a ventral gondola or with provision for carriage of two torpedoes for anti-shipping missions.

Heinkel He 177A-5

While the proposed He 177A-4 high-altitude version never made it into service, the next variant to join the Luftwaffe was the He 177A-5 that featured structural modifications, including a strengthened wing intended to support heavier underwing loads. The He 177A-5/R1 to He 177A-5/R4 featured minor changes in armament, while the He 177A-5/R5 introduced a remotely-controlled defensive barbette to the rear of the weapons bays. The He 177A-5/R7 was equipped with a pressurized cockpit, while the He 177A-5/R8 was fitted with barbettes in the chin and rear positions. A small number of He 177A-5s were also converted for the *Zerstörer* role, with the bomb bays modified to accommodate an array

Heinkel He 177A-5/R-2
Another example of the He 177A-5/R2 sub-variant, 6N+BN was assigned to 5./Kampfgeschwader 100, operating in Denmark, in summer 1944.

of 33 rocket tubes arranged to fire upwards at an angle of 60 degrees.

Improved defensive armament

Further efforts were made to improve the defensive capabilities of the bomber, resulting in the He 177A-6. Only six He 177A-6/R1 development aircraft were produced for a variant that incorporated additional armament and armour protection for the crew compartment and fuel tanks. One of the development aircraft was tested with a redesigned forward fuselage and heavier armament for the proposed He 177A-6/R2.

Heinkel He 177A-5/R-2
Weight (Maximum take-off) 31,000kg (68,300lb)
Dimensions Length: 22m (72ft 2in), Wingspan: 31.44m (103ft 2in), Height: 6.4m (21ft)
Powerplant Two 2133kW (2860hp) Daimler-Benz DB 610 24-cylinder liquid-cooled piston engines
Speed 565km/h (351mph)
Range 1540km (960 miles)
Ceiling 8000m (26,000ft)
Crew 6
Armament One 7.92mm (0.31) MG 81 machine gun (nose), two 20mm (0.8in) MG 151 cannon (forward ventral gondola and tail), four 13mm (0.51in) MG 131 machine guns (rear gondola, forward dorsal turret, aft dorsal turret); 16 50kg (110lb) SC 50, four 250kg (551lb) SC 250 or two 500kg (1102lb) SC 500, or two LMA III parachute sea mines, LT 50 torpedos or Hs 293 missiles

An He 177 is serviced and bombed-up prior to flying a mission.

BOMBERS

Work was meanwhile underway on the He 177A-7, with a revised wingspan of 36m (118ft). A total of six He 177A-5s were modified to test the new wing, but with DB 610 engines instead of the proposed 2685kW (3600hp) DB 613 units.

Night bombers

Small numbers of He 177A-5s returned to nocturnal bombing raids over the UK in early 1944 and the type also saw service on the Eastern Front, where He 177A-3s were used to resupply the Wehrmacht forces under siege at Stalingrad in January 1943.

However, the increasing demand for fighters for defence of the Reich meant

Heinkel He 177A-5/R-6

V4+KN was an example of the He 177A-5/R-6 sub-variant, flown by 5./Kampfgeschwader 1. It was active in East Prussia during June 1944.

that the Heinkel bomber was never afforded priority status, and by the end of 1944 the type had effectively been withdrawn from service.

Had Nazi Germany succeeded in producing a practical nuclear bomb, the He 177 would have been the likely carrier, and a single example (He 177 V38) was being modified for this role in Prague as the war came to an end.

In total, production amounted to around 1160 aircraft in addition to some 30 prototypes.

Heinkel He 177A-5/R-6
Weight (Maximum take-off) 31,000kg (68,300lb)
Dimensions Length: 22m (72ft 2in), Wingspan: 31.44m (103ft 2in), Height: 6.4m (21ft)
Powerplant Two 2133kW (2860hp) Daimler-Benz DB 610 24-cylinder liquid-cooled piston engines
Speed 565km/h (351mph)
Range 1540km (960 miles)
Ceiling 8000m (26,000ft)
Crew 6
Armament One 7.92mm (0.31in) MG 81 machine gun (nose), two 20mm (0.8in) MG 151 cannon (forward ventral gondola and tail), four 13mm (0.51in) MG 131 machine guns (rear gondola, forward dorsal turret, aft dorsal turret); up to 7000kg (15,000lb) of ordnance internally, up to 2500kg (5500lb) externally on underwing racks

Most He 177 sub-types had an MG 151/20 in the front of the gondola and a second in the tail, aimed by the gunner who sat under the plexiglas bulge under the rudder.

BOMBERS

Messerschmitt Me 264

The Me 264 emerged from Messerschmitt's research into creating a four-engine long-range bomber that began during 1940.

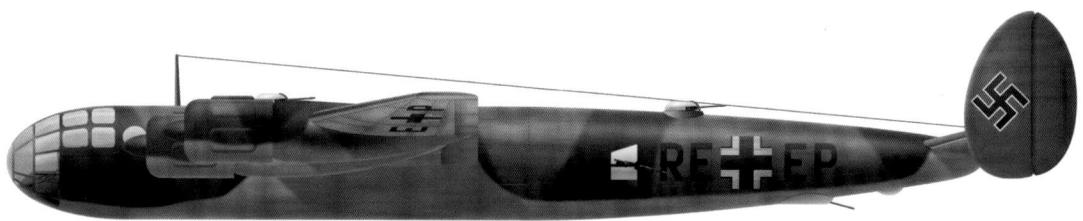

The design team selected an aerodynamically clean, high-wing cantilever monoplane configuration and the aircraft was provided with retractable tricycle undercarriage, each unit featuring a single wheel with very large tyres. The tail unit included twin canted fins and rudders. The powerplant made use of four 999kW (1340hp) Junkers Jumo 211J-1 engines and in this form the first prototype Me 264 V1 performed a maiden flight in December 1942.

Long-range limits

The entry of the United States to the war prompted official interest in a strategic bomber with the range to reach North American targets from bases in Europe, and the Me 264 was no longer able to meet this *Amerika-Bomber* requirement. The company planned a six-engine version able to carry a heavier payload, but the *Reichsluftfahrtministerium* (German Air Ministry) preferred the Junkers Ju 390 – itself a further development of the Ju 290 transport. In the event, a development contract went to Junkers, but not before another two Me 264 prototypes had been ordered for evaluation in the long-range reconnaissance role. The Allied bombing campaign and a shortage of raw materials meant neither of these aircraft was completed. Had they been built, prototypes Me 264 V1 and V2 would have been powered by BMW 801D or G radial engines and were expected to offer a range of 15,000km (9321 miles).

Escape airplane

In an interesting postscript to the programme, the sole Me 264 V1 – which had mainly been used as an aerodynamic testbed – was apparently readied to transport Adolf Hitler to Japan should the army generals' July 1944 plot to overthrow the leader have succeeded.

Messerschmitt 264 V3

The third prototype, Me 264 V3, wore the registration RE+EP, and represented the standard for the pre-production A-0 series. It was incomplete when the programme was cancelled in 1944.

Messerschmitt 264 V3
Weight (Maximum take-off) 21,150kg (46,627lb)
Dimensions Length: 20.9m (68ft 6.75in), Wingspan: 43m (141ft 1in), Height: 4.3m (14ft 1.25in)
Powerplant Four 1250kW (1677hp) BMW 801D radial engines
Speed 546km/h (339mph)
Range 15,000km (9321 miles)
Ceiling 8000m (26,250ft)
Crew 8
Armament Four 13mm (0.51in) MG 131 machine guns, two 20mm (0.8in) MG 151/20 cannons; 3000kg (6614lb) internal bombload

Junkers Ju 188

Intended as the successor to the prolific Ju 88, the design of the Ju 188 was already well advanced by the outbreak of World War II when the company had examined a potentially stretched Ju 85B and Ju 88B.

However, by 1942 it was apparent that the programme was suffering delays and a stopgap aircraft would be required to begin supplanting the Ju 88 in the short term. This emerged from the Ju 88B, first flown in 1940 and which introduced a new crew compartment with more extensively glazed nose, increased-span wings and a revised powerplant of two 1193kW (1600hp) BMW 801MA radial engines.

In the event, only 10 pre-production Ju 88B-0 aircraft were built, since the B-series was not judged to offer a considerable improvement over the original Ju 88A, with which it otherwise shared commonality.

Next-generation medium bomber

However, the Ju 88B was not an evolutionary dead-end and led directly to the Ju 88E, including a pre-series batch of Ju 88E-0 aircraft that became the basis for the Ju 188 four-seat bomber/reconnaissance aircraft. This was selected as the Luftwaffe's next-generation medium bomber, beating off competition from the Dornier Do 317, Focke-Wulf Fw 191 and Junkers Ju 288.

En route to the definitive Ju 188, the company continued to refine the Ju 88, including the Ju 88 V27 prototype that combined a Ju 88E-0 airframe with extended outer wings with new pointed tips. Further refinements appeared in the Ju 88 V44, with enlarged tail, increased-span tailplane and larger fin and rudder – both now being more rectangular in shape.

The first 'true' prototype for the new aircraft, the Ju 188 V1, was the re-designated Ju 88 V44 that had first flown in spring 1942. A second prototype, the Ju 188 V2, took to the air in January 1943, and the type was authorized for production after successfully completing evaluation.

From the outset, the Ju 188 was intended to be suitable for either BMW

Junkers Ju 188A-3

Wearing the 'Wellenmuster' camouflage pattern typical for operations in the Mediterranean Sea, this Ju 188A-3 was flown by III./Kampfgeschwader 26, in April 1945.

Junkers Ju 188A-3

Weight (Maximum take-off) 14,510kg (31,989lb)
Dimensions Length: 14.9m (49ft 0.5in), Wingspan: 22m (72ft 2in), Height: 4.45m (14ft 7in)
Powerplant Two 1290kW (1730hp) Jumo 213A-1 radial engines
Speed 499km/h (310mph)
Range 2400km (1490 miles)
Ceiling 9347m (30,665ft)
Crew 4
Armament One 20mm (0.8in) MG 151/20 cannon (dorsal turret), two 13mm (0.5in) MG 131 machine guns; FuG 200 Hohentwiel sea-search radar; provision for 3000kg (6600lb) bombload

BOMBERS

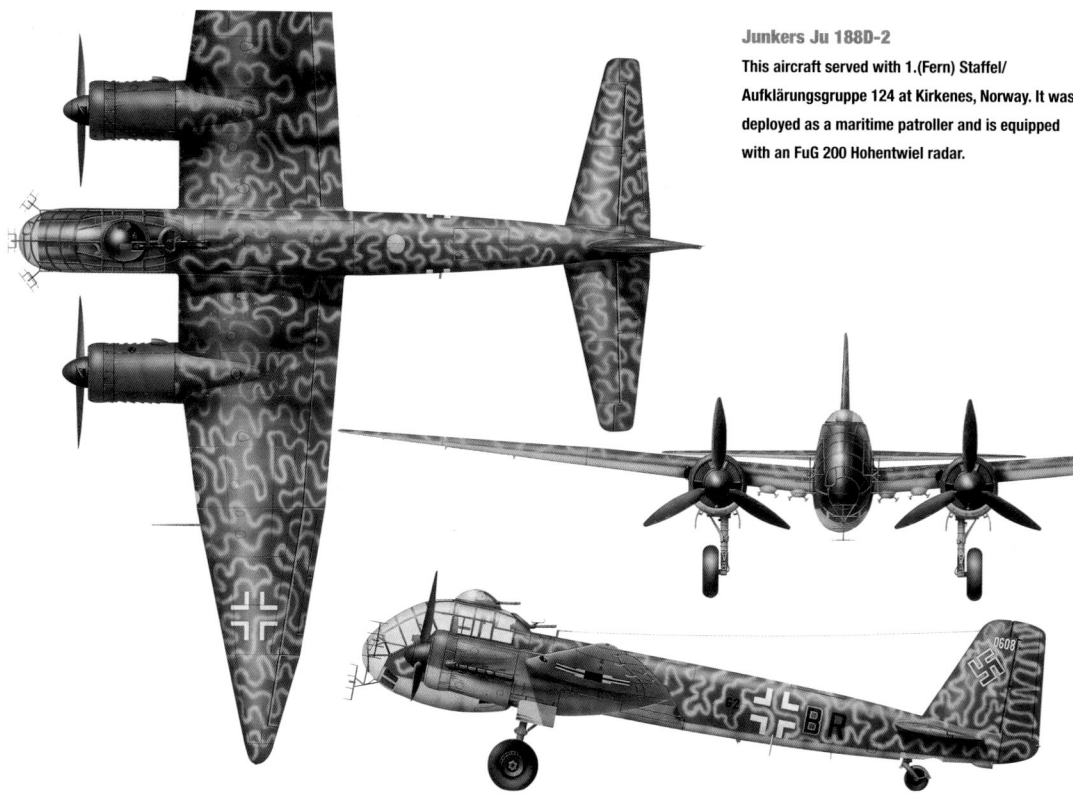

Junkers Ju 188D-2
This aircraft served with 1.(Fern) Staffel/ Aufklärungsgruppe 124 at Kirkenes, Norway. It was deployed as a maritime patroller and is equipped with an FuG 200 Hohentwiel radar.

801 or Junkers Jumo 213 engines, to ensure that production wouldn't be interrupted by a shortage of either one of these powerplants.

Junkers Ju 188E-1

While it was originally anticipated that production would begin with the Jumo-engine Ju 188A-1 bomber, in the event the aircraft was launched into series production in Ju 188E-1 form, a bomber version powered by a pair of 1193kW (1600hp) BMW 801ML engines. This entered Luftwaffe service with Ekdo d.Lw 188 and KG 6 in May 1943 and by the end of the same year, 283 examples had been completed. The first of the operational Gruppe was I./KG 6, which began flying pathfinder missions on 20 October 1943. The E-series continued with the Ju 188E-2 torpedo-bomber for anti-shipping operations.

Junkers Ju 188D-2
Weight (Maximum take-off) 14,510kg (31,989lb)
Dimensions Length: 14.9m (49ft 0.5in), Wingspan: 22m (72ft 2in), Height: 4.45m (14ft 7in)
Powerplant Two 1193kW (1600hp) BMW 801ML radial engines
Speed 499km/h (310mph)
Range 3400km (2110 miles)
Ceiling 9347m (30,665ft)
Crew 4
Armament Two 13mm (0.5in) MG 131 machine guns; FuG 200 Hohentwiel sea-search radar; provision for 3000kg (6600lb) bombload

The first major production version with the Junkers powerplant was the Ju 188A-2 bomber, which featured two Jumo 213A-1 engines that each developed 1670kW (2240hp) for take-off with water/methanol injection. Other subvariants of the A-series included the Ju 188A-3 with provision for torpedo carriage under the inner wings. While the Ju 188E-1 featured defensive armament in the form of a dorsal turret with a 13mm (0.51in) MG 131 machine gun, the A-series made use of the 20mm (0.8in) MG 151/20 cannon and featured improved performance overall, especially when equipped with the MW50 power-boosting system.

In an attempt to improve the defensive armament, Junkers tested the Ju 188C-0 with a remotely sighted and power-operated tail barbette fitted with a twin MG 131Z machine gun, but results were poor and this series was consequently abandoned.

D and G series

The D-series encompassed the Ju 188D-1 and D-2, both of which were equipped for reconnaissance duties and which had no forward-firing MG 151 cannon, in a bid to improve high-altitude performance. Other changes included a three-man crew and additional fuel capacity. The Ju 188D-2 version was differentiated by its FuG 200 radar fitted for maritime operations. The Ju 188F series, meanwhile, included the Ju 188F-1 and Ju 188F-2 – these were equivalent to the Ju 188D-1 and D-2, but incorporated the alternative BMW powerplant.

The Ju 188G-0 introduced defensive armament to cover the rear sector in the form of a small manned MG 131 installation, but the results were unsatisfactory. Instead, the twin MG 131Z tail gun was installed in the Ju 188G-2 bomber and the Ju 188H-1 reconnaissance aircraft.

High-altitude model

In autumn 1943 work began on a high-altitude Ju 188 development with a pressurized crew compartment. This was planned to be produced as the Ju 188J heavy fighter, Ju 188K bomber and Ju 188I reconnaissance aircraft. Such were the changes, however, that the

The Ju 88 V44 was the second of the Ju 188 development vehicles and introduced the enlarged tail surfaces. As such, it was redesignated as the Ju 188 V1 during mid-1942.

BOMBERS

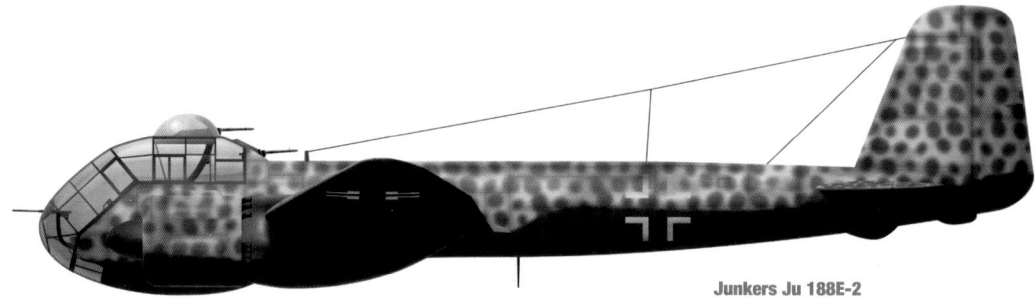

Junkers Ju 188E-2
This Ju 188E-2 was flown by Kampfgeschwader 6 during Operation Steinbock, the 'mini Blitz' that targeted southern England in spring 1944.

Reichsluftfahrtministerium (German Air Ministry) assigned the new designation Ju 388 in September 1943.

In the same way in which Junkers developed Ju 88S high-altitude intruder and Ju 88T reconnaissance versions of the Ju 88, the Ju 188 that followed was also refined for work at higher altitudes, resulting in the Ju 188S-1 high-altitude intruder and the Ju 188T-1 high-altitude reconnaissance aircraft. These combined the pressurized forward fuselage that had been developed under the Ju 388 programme with the existing Ju 188 airframe. Neither of these versions featured defensive armament and both were powered by a pair of Jumo 213E-1 engines fitted with GM-1 nitrous oxide power boosting to provide 1260kW (1690hp) at 9570m (31,400ft).

Both S and T-series entered production in early 1944 but neither was produced in significant quantities. By the end of the same year, Ju 188S-1 aircraft were having their pressurization equipment removed and were being adapted for the ground-attack role. These aircraft were known under the Ju 188S-1/U designation and were normally flown by a crew of two.

Reconnaissance role

In all, more than 1000 Ju 188s of all variants were completed and more than half of these were destined to serve in the reconnaissance role. While the aircraft had only a limited impact on the war, it was judged to be superior to the Ju 88 in most respects, with improved handling – especially at high operating weights.

The course of the war meant that the reconnaissance Ju 188s achieved only very limited success, while the bomber variants saw most of their service in the anti-shipping role, especially in Denmark and Norway.

This Junkers Ju 188E-1 is equipped with a FuG 200 Hohentwiel radar, which was capable of detecting ships up to a distance of 10km (6.2 miles).

Junkers Ju 188E-2
Weight (Maximum take-off) 14,510kg (31,989lb)
Dimensions Length: 14.9m (49ft 0.5in), Wingspan: 22m (72ft 2in), Height: 4.45m (14ft 7in)
Powerplant Powerplant Two 1290kW (1730hp) Jumo 213A-1 radial engines with GM-1 nitrous oxide power boost
Speed 499km/h (310mph)
Range 2400km (1490 miles)
Ceiling 9570m (31,400ft)
Crew 4
Armament One 20mm (0.8in) MG 151/20 cannon (dorsal turret), three 13mm (0.51in) MG 131 machine guns; 3000kg (6600lb) bombload

Arado Ar 234 *Blitz*

The world's first jet-powered bomber began life in late 1940 when work was launched at Arado on a fast reconnaissance aircraft in response to a requirement issued by the German Air Ministry.

Arado Ar 234B-1
The first Arado Ar 234s were delivered to specially set-up *Sonderkommando*, where they were used for reconnaissance.

The manufacturer's design team was led by Walter Blume and Hans Rebeski, who drafted a project designated E.370. Once scaled up, this emerged in prototype form in early 1943 as the Ar 234. The aircraft utilized a shoulder-wing configuration with engines under the wings. The fuselage was notably narrow, such that it was unable to accommodate an conventional undercarriage. Instead, it was provided with a jettisonable take-off trolley and retractable skids on which to return to its airfield.

The planned Junkers turbojets were delayed, the first test examples arriving at Warnemünde in February 1943, where they were installed in the first prototype that began taxi trials in March. This pushed back the aircraft's maiden flight to 15 June 1943. The aircraft first flew from Rheine under the power of a pair of 840kg (1852lb) thrust Jumo 004B-0 engines, the first flight-cleared examples of which arrived at the base in May.

It was soon discovered that the schemed undercarriage arrangement was less than practical. As envisaged, the aircraft jettisoned its take-off trolley at a height of 60 metres (195ft), and this was to be recovered after returning to earth under five braking parachutes. After parachute failures destroyed the first two trolleys, the configuration was revised, and the trolley was instead released immediately after take-off.

Trolley undercarriage

The trolley-undercarriage version was the Ar 234A; also completed to this standard, the third prototype flew on 22 August 1943 and added rocket-assisted take-off (RATO) gear together with a pressurized cockpit with ejector seat. It was followed by the fifth and sixth prototypes, which flew on 15 September and 20 December respectively. Next into the air was the eighth prototype, this aircraft introducing a four-engine powerplant consisting of 800kg (1764lb) thrust BMW 003A-1 engines in paired nacelles. The sixth prototype followed it into the air on 8 April 1944, this time powered by four BMW 003A-1s

Arado Ar 234B-1
Weight (Maximum take-off) 9800kg (21,560lb)
Dimensions Length: 12.64m (41ft), Wingspan: 14.44m (46ft), Height: 4.29m (14ft)
Powerplant Two 8.8kN (1975lbf) Junkers Jumo 004B-1 Orkan turbojet engines
Speed 742km/h (460mph)
Range 1630km (1010 miles)
Ceiling 10,000m (33,000ft)
Crew 1
Armament Two Rb 50/30 or Rb 75/30 cameras; maximum bombload 1500kg (3310lb)

BOMBERS

arranged in four separate nacelles. In the meantime, work continued to improve the Jumo 004B engine and the seventh and last of the Ar 234A prototypes received these units, now developing 980kg (1962lb) of thrust. However, this seventh prototype crashed after an engine fire, claiming the life of Arado's chief test pilot.

Finally, the original undercarriage concept was abandoned after it had become clear that it was simply too difficult to move the Ar 234 around on the ground prior to loading it on its launch trolley. In response, the company developed the Ar 234B with a moderately widened fuselage that would accommodate retractable landing gear. The ninth prototype was duly equipped with the new undercarriage and first flew on 10 March 1944. The design moved a step closer to a practical operational aircraft with the next – tenth – prototype, equipped with bomb racks below the engine nacelles and a bomb-aiming computer; however, the cabin pressurization was deleted.

B series prototype

The remaining B-series prototypes included the 13th, notable for being powered by two pairs of BMW 003A-1 engines, and aircraft 15 and 17, each with two of the BMW engines and which were used as testbeds to rectify thrust control problems with this powerplant. The four-engine BMW 003A-1 version was productionised as the Ar 234C, the 19th prototype being completed to this standard and first flown on 30 September 1944.

The 20 Ar 234B-0 pre-production machines were mainly employed for continued test work at Rechlin and were generally without either

Arado-Ar-234B-2

Weight (Maximum take-off) 9800kg (21,560lb)
Dimensions Length: 12.64m (41ft), Wingspan: 14.44m (46ft), Height: 4.29m (14ft)
Powerplant Two 8.8kN (1975lbf) Junkers Jumo 004B-1 Orkan turbojet engines, plus two Walter HWK 109-500A-1 Starthilfe liquid fuelled jettisonable JATO rocket pods
Speed 742km/h (460mph)
Range 1630km (1010 miles)
Ceiling 10,000m (33,000ft)
Crew 1
Armament 2000kg (4409lb) maximum bombload

Arado Ar 232B-2
Shown carrying its external bombload, Ar 234B-2 *Werknummer* 140456 of 8./Kampfgeschwader 76 was shot down near Bohmke, Germany, on 25 February 1945.

Arado Ar 234B-2
Ar 234B-2 *Werknummer* 140312 was one of nine Ar 234s surrendered to British forces at Sola airfield near Stavanger, Norway. The aircraft had been operating with 8./Kampfgeschwader 76 (later reorganised as an *Einsatzstaffel*).

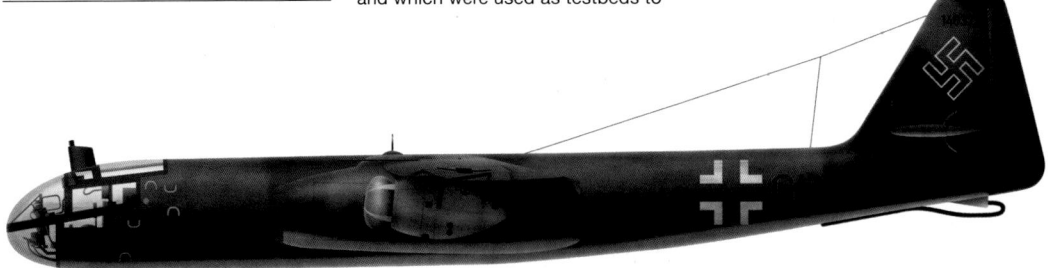

BOMBERS

pressurization systems or ejection seats. Although the take-off trolley had been abandoned for the long term, in the meantime prototypes five and seven – equipped with Walter RATO gear – were diverted to operational evaluation by the 1./Versuchsverband Oberbefehlhaber der Luftwaffe, stationed at Juvincourt, France. Despite their shortcomings on the ground, these aircraft demonstrated excellent performance in the air and completed numerous sorties over Allied territory unmolested by enemy fighters.

Production model

The production-standard Ar 234B-1 was produced in only small numbers but was issued to experimental reconnaissance units, *Sonderkommandos Götz*, *Hecht*, *Sperlin* and *Sommer*. Another two units, the 1.(F)/33 and 1.(F)/100 were also operational with small numbers of the type at the end of the war. While these all involved reconnaissance versions, equipped with a pair of cameras, the bomber Ar 234B-2 derivative became operational with the Stabstaffel of KG 76. The Ar 234B-2 could carry a maximum bombload of 2000kg (4409lb) on ETC 503 bomb racks below the engine nacelles.

Another operator was the *Kommando Bonow*, which received a handful of aircraft for experimental night fighter work. Night fighter developments of the basic airframe yielded the Ar 234C-3/N proposal with two forward-firing 20mm (0.81in) MG 151/20 cannon and two 30mm (1.18in) MK 108 cannon and with FuG 218 Neptun V radar. The similar Ar 234C-7 would have had side-by-side seating for the crew and improved FuG 245 Bremen 0 centimetric radar.

Four-engine versions of the production Ar 234B-1 (recce) and Ar

Arado 234s line up, awaiting another mission during the Ardennes offensive of December 1944. The Arado 234 was used for pinpoint attacks on Allied ground positions.

BOMBERS

234B-2 (bomber) emerged as the Ar 234C-1 and C-2 respectively, with the former featuring full pressurization for the cabin and defensive armament in the form of two rearward-firing MG 151/20 cannons.

The Ar 234C-3, meanwhile, was intended to be a multi-purpose version, and was tested by prototypes 21 to 25. These all featured redesigned cockpits

with a raised profile. Armament was the same as that for the Ar 234C-1, but with an additional pair of MG 151/20s beneath the nose. A variety of disposable stores could be carried on three ETC 504 bomb racks.

Other versions that failed to be fielded included the Ar 234C-4 armed reconnaissance version with two cameras and four MG 151/20s; the Ar 234C-5 (28th prototype) with side-by-side seating for pilot and bomb-aimer; and the Ar 234C-6 two-seat reconnaissance aircraft (29th prototype). Had the 1080kg (2381lb) thrust Jumo 004D engine been available in time, it would have powered the proposed Ar 234C-8 single-seat bomber, while the Heinkel-Hirth HeS 011A, developing 1300kg (2865lb), was envisaged for the Ar 234D series, prototypes for which (31 to 40) were being completed when the war came to an end.

Arado-Ar-234C-3
Weight (Maximum take-off) 9800kg (21,560lb)
Dimensions Length: 12.64m (41ft), Wingspan: 14.44m (46ft), Height: 4.29m (14ft)
Powerplant Four 7.8kN (1760lbf) BMW 003A axial turbojets
Speed 742km/h (460mph)
Range 1630km (1010 miles)
Ceiling 10,000m (33,000ft)
Crew 1
Armament Two forward-firing 20mm (0.81in) MG 151/20 cannon and two 30mm (1.18in) MK 108 cannon; maximum bombload of 1500kg (3307lb)

Arado-Ar-234B-2/N
Converted as one of two night fighter prototypes, Ar 234B-2/N *Werknummer* 140145 crashed on 13 February 1945 at Oranienburg, Germany. Note the twin 20mm (0.8in) MG 151/20 cannon mounted in a ventral pod.

Arado-Ar-234B-2/N
Weight (Maximum take-off) 9800kg (21,560lb)
Dimensions Length: 12.64m (41ft), Wingspan: 14.44m (46ft), Height: 4.29m (14ft)
Powerplant Four 7.8kN (1760lbf) BMW 003A axial turbojets
Speed 742km/h (460mph)
Range 1630km (1010 miles)
Ceiling 10,000m (33,000ft)
Crew 2
Armament Two forward-firing 20mm (0.8in) MG 151/20 autocannon within a *Magirusbombe* conformal gun pod; FuG 218 'Neptun' VHF-band radar

Arado-Ar-234C-3
This Ar 234C-3, *Werknummer* 250012, was captured by the Red Army at Prague in May 1945.

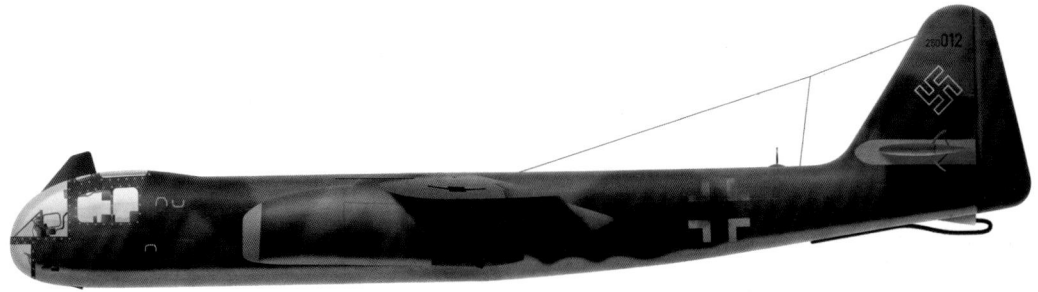

BOMBERS

Fieseler Fi 103R *Reichenberg*

A piloted version of the famous V-1 flying bomb, the Fi 103R *Reichenberg* was intended for precision attacks on high-priority targets and began to be considered a practical proposition in late 1943.

The original V-1 was a fixed-wing, pilotless aircraft powered by an Argus pulsejet engine mounted above the rear fuselage and incorporated a simple flight control system to guide it to the target. An air-log system was installed to calculate the correct distance from launch to target, based on a pre-set distance, at which point the motor would cut out and the missile would began a terminal dive. A high-explosive warhead was fitted. The first raid was mounted against London on 13 June 1944.

Ahead of this, the piloted V-1 was given the go-ahead by Adolf Hitler in March 1944, using the same Fi 103 airframe and given the codename *Reichenberg*.

Planned versions

There were four planned versions of the Fi 103R: an unpowered Fi 103R-I for initial flight tests; powered Fi 103R-II and R-III two-seat models for basic and advanced training respectively; and the definitive Fi 103R-IV for operational missions. The Fi 103R-IV was intended for launch from a mother plane, the pilot employing conventional controls and control surfaces to reach the target. After making a final aim at

Fieseler Fi 103R Reichenberg
After aiming his missile at the target, the Reichenberg pilot was expected to bale out. This action was almost certain to result in him being sucked into the engine intake.

the objective, the pilot was expected to bale out by parachute.

Around 175 examples of the Fi 103R were eventually completed, but the project was cancelled in late 1944 before any of the manned V-1s could be employed in combat.

Fieseler Fi 103R-IV Reichenberg
Weight (Maximum take-off) 2250kg (4960lb)
Dimensions Length: 5.72m (18ft 9in), Wingspan: 8m (26ft 3in)
Powerplant One 2.9kN (660lbf) Argus As 109-014 pulsejet
Speed 650km/h (400mph) at 2400m (8000ft)
Range 329km (204 miles)
Endurance 32 minutes
Crew 1
Armament 850kg (1874lb) high-explosive warhead

A British civilian examines the wreckage of a crashed 'Doodlebug' V-1 Flying Bomb somewhere in southern England, 1944.

GROUND-ATTACK AND RECONNAISSANCE AIRCRAFT

GROUND-ATTACK AND RECONNAISSANCE AIRCRAFT

Ground-attack aircraft played a vital role in the victorious German campaigns of 1939–41. The German Army's *blitzkrieg* ('lightning war') doctrine involved close integration of tactical air power and mechanized infantry units, and this combination of Panzer mobility and airborne artillery was, for a while, unstoppable.

This chapter includes the following aircraft:

- Henschel Hs 123
- Junkers Ju 87
- Henschel Hs 126
- Fieseler Fi 156 *Storch*
- Focke-Wulf Fw 189 *Uhu*
- Henschel Hs 129
- Henschel Hs 132
- Blohm und Voss BV 141

Junkers Ju 87 Stukas set out on a mission somewhere on the Eastern Front. The Ju 87 was effective in the early stages of the invasion of the Soviet Union, but by 1943 mounting losses meant they were switched to night-time operations.

GROUND-ATTACK AND RECONNAISSANCE AIRCRAFT

Henschel Hs 123

The Hs 123 was designed to meet a 1934 requirement for a dive-bomber but was destined to see more extensive service as a close-support aircraft.

The requirement as originally drafted called for a two-stage programme, of which the Hs 123 would meet the first (interim) stage, before a monoplane dive-bomber became available. The first of three protypes of the unequal-span biplane (sesquiplane) took to the air in spring 1935 powered by a 485kW (650hp) BMW 132A-3 nine-cylinder radial engine and the type soon demonstrated its superiority over the rival Fieseler Fi 98 design.

Beginning in August 1935, the first three aircraft were subjected to tests at Rechlin, where two of them were lost after their wings suffered structural failure in dives. The fourth prototype introduced structural changes to address these shortcomings, and in this form the aircraft was ordered into production.

Standard armament for the series-built aircraft comprised a pair of forward-firing 7.92mm (0.31in) MG 17 machine guns, plus provision for up to 450kg (992lb) of bombs: typically, a single 250kg (551lb) bomb carried on a centreline crutch that swung forward between the main wheels, and up to four 50kg (110lb) bombs on wing racks.

The initial series-production Hs 123A-1 variant entered service with I./Sturzkampfgeschwader 162 'Immelmann' in summer 1936 but it was destined for only a brief frontline career as a dive-bomber as deliveries of the Junkers Ju 87A monoplane began the following year. In December 1936, five Hs 123As were sent to Spain for operational trials with the Condor Legion.

Improvements to the basic design were made in the fifth and sixth prototypes, the Hs 123 V5 and V6, both of which were powered by a 716kW (960hp) BMW 132K engine and which featured revised armament. However, the planned Hs 123B (with BMW 132K and long-chord cowling) and Hs 123C (additional machine guns and armoured headrest) did not enter production.

Combat service

During World War II, the Hs 123 saw combat service during the invasion of Poland in September 1939, but by this stage only a single frontline unit remained equipped with the type: II

Henschel Hs 123A-1

This early machine was based at Fürstenfeldbruck with 7./Stukageschwader 165 'Immelmann' during October 1937.

Henschel Hs 123A-1

Weight (Maximum take-off) 2215kg (4883lb)
Dimensions Length: 8.33m (27ft 4in), Wingspan: 10.5m (34ft 5in), Height: 3.2m (10ft 6in)
Powerplant One 716kW (960hp) BMW 132K engine
Speed 341km/h (212mph)
Range 860km (530 miles)
Ceiling 9000m (30,000ft)
Crew 1
Armament Two forward-firing 7.92mm (0.31in) MG 17 machine guns; one 250kg (551lb) bomb, plus four 50kg (110lb) bombs on wing racks

(Schlacht)./Lehrgeschwader 2. The biplane was judged a resounding success in the Polish campaign and plans to re-equip the unit were put on hold. Thereafter, the Hs 123 was involved in the campaigns in Belgium and France in 1940.

After a period spent in the Balkans from April 1941, the Hs 123s were incorporated within the newly formed

GROUND-ATTACK AND RECONNAISSANCE AIRCRAFT

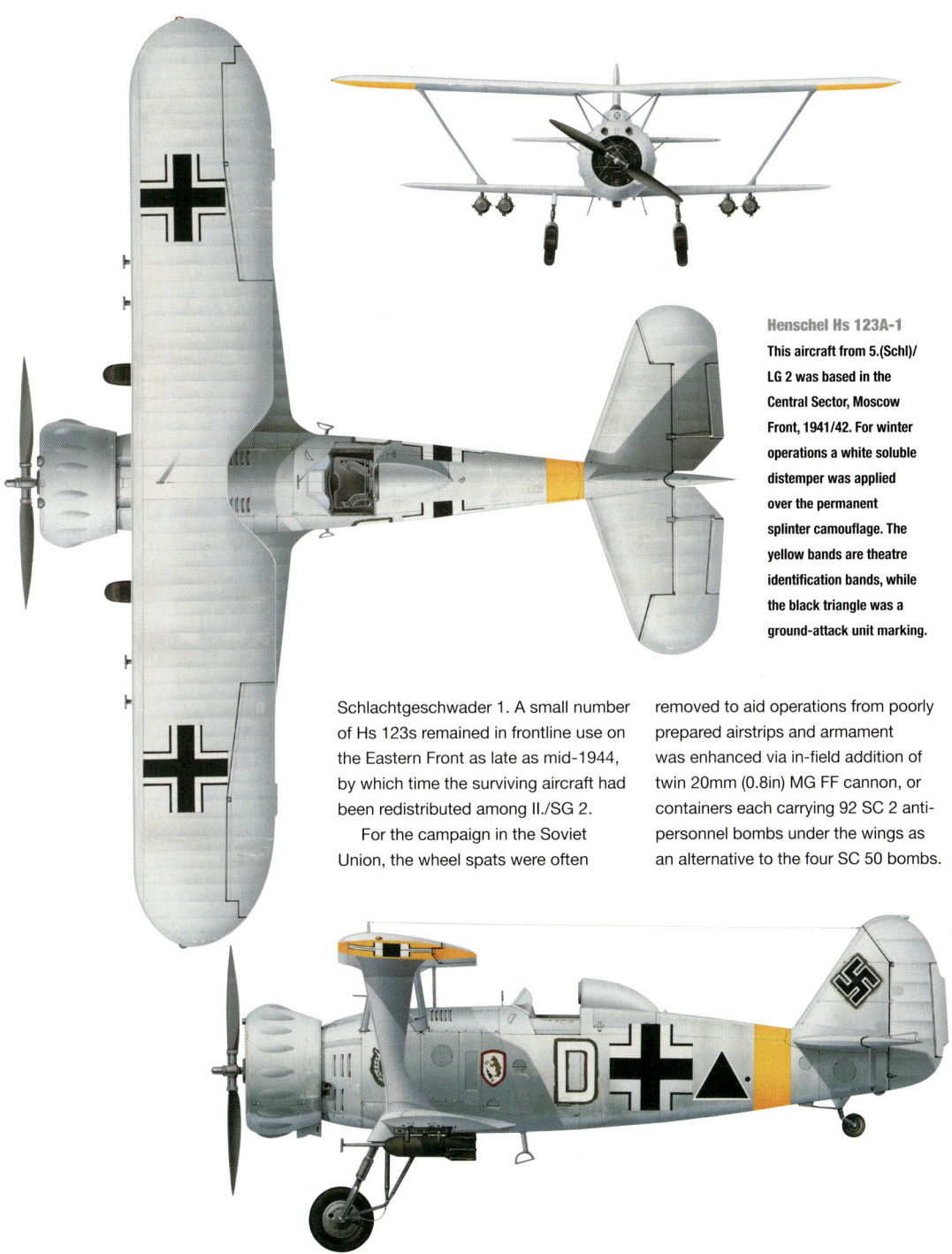

Henschel Hs 123A-1
This aircraft from 5.(Schl)/LG 2 was based in the Central Sector, Moscow Front, 1941/42. For winter operations a white soluble distemper was applied over the permanent splinter camouflage. The yellow bands are theatre identification bands, while the black triangle was a ground-attack unit marking.

Schlachtgeschwader 1. A small number of Hs 123s remained in frontline use on the Eastern Front as late as mid-1944, by which time the surviving aircraft had been redistributed among II./SG 2.

For the campaign in the Soviet Union, the wheel spats were often removed to aid operations from poorly prepared airstrips and armament was enhanced via in-field addition of twin 20mm (0.8in) MG FF cannon, or containers each carrying 92 SC 2 anti-personnel bombs under the wings as an alternative to the four SC 50 bombs.

55

GROUND-ATTACK AND RECONNAISSANCE AIRCRAFT

Junkers Ju 87

Emblematic of the rapid advances made by the German Army in the Polish campaign, the Ju 87 was relatively quickly withdrawn from operations over Western Europe after meeting concerted fighter opposition.

Junkers Ju 87A-1

Wearing Spanish Nationalist markings, this Ju 87A-1 fought as part of the Condor Legion in Spain, assigned to the Luftwaffe's 5./Kampfgruppe 88, in 1938.

However, the Ju 87 continued to perform usefully on the Eastern Front well into 1943. Better known as the Stuka (for *Sturzkampfflugzeug*, or 'dive-bomber'), the Ju 87 began life in prototype form in 1934. Its design was heavily influenced by Junkers' work on the K 47, a single-engined, low-wing monoplane with fixed undercarriage and twin fins and rudders that was first flown in 1928.

The first of three Ju 87 prototypes was similarly equipped with twin vertical tail surfaces and powered by a Rolls-Royce Kestrel engine. This initial aircraft was destroyed during dive tests in 1935 when the tail unit collapsed and the second aircraft adopted a single fin and rudder, as well as a 455kW (610hp) Junkers Jumo 210A engine. Evaluation of the second and a further improved third prototype led to a pre-production batch of 10 Ju 87A-0 aircraft, now with the Jumo 210Ca rated at 477kW (640hp).

The initial-production Ju 87A-1 began to replace the Henschel Hs 123 biplane from spring 1937 and three examples went to Spain for combat evaluation with the Condor Legion. Once in Spain, the Stuka achieved excellent results in combat and an equal measure of notoriety, aided by the decision to attach sirens – so-called 'Trumpets of Jericho' – to the landing gear, for a significant psychological effect on those it was targeting. The improved Ju 87A-2 subvariant was the next production model, this time with a supercharged 500kW (680hp) Jumo 210Da engine.

First combat

By the outbreak of World War II, the Luftwaffe had a total of 336 of the improved Ju 87B aircraft on strength, and production had reached a rate of up to 60 aircraft per month. The Ju 87B had begun life as prototype Ju 87 V7, introducing the new Jumo 211A engine, rated at 735kW (1000hp).

After a pre-series batch of Ju 87B-0 aircraft, manufacturing output switched to the Ju 87B-1 that featured

Junkers Ju 87A-1
Weight (Maximum take-off) 3400kg (7495lb)
Dimensions Length: 10.78m (35ft 4in), Wingspan: 13.8m (45ft 3in), Height: 3.89m (12ft 8in)
Powerplant One 455kW (610hp) Junkers Jumo 210A engine
Speed 320km/h (199mph)
Range 1000km (620 miles)
Ceiling 7000m (22,965ft)
Crew 2
Armament Two 7.92mm (0.31in) MG 17 machine guns (forward firing), one 7.92mm (0.31in) MG 15 machine gun (cockpit rear); 500kg (1102lb) bombload

a redesigned fuselage and streamlined wheel spats. Its powerplant was the further up-rated Jumo 211Da developing 882kW (1200hp) and it was able to carry a bombload of 500kg (1102lb). Offensive firepower was further improved in the Ju 87B-2, which was able to carry 1000kg (2205lb) of external stores. It was the Ju 87B-1 that flew the Luftwaffe's first combat mission of the war, when examples attacked the bridge over the Vistula

GROUND-ATTACK AND RECONNAISSANCE AIRCRAFT

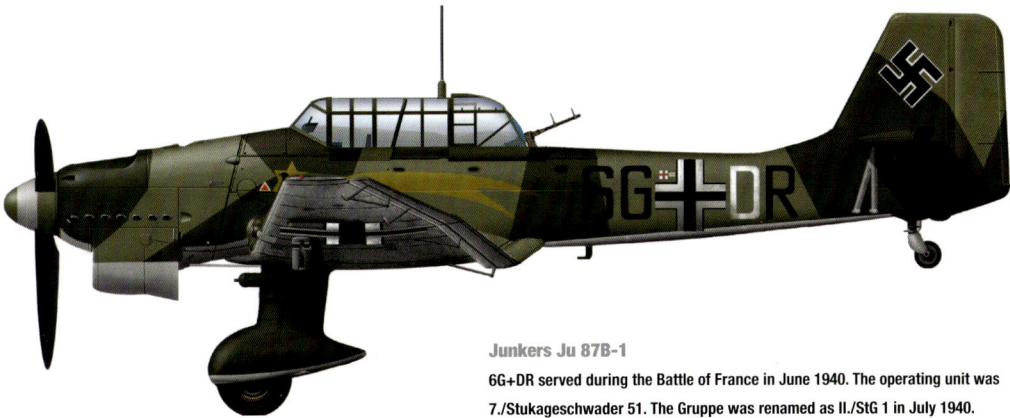

Junkers Ju 87B-1

6G+DR served during the Battle of France in June 1940. The operating unit was 7./Stukageschwader 51. The Gruppe was renamed as II./StG 1 in July 1940.

river at Dirschau, on 1 September 1939. The Ju 87 was successful throughout the campaign in Poland, attacking troop concentrations and being credited with sinking all but two of Poland's warships.

The Ju 87C was envisaged for shipborne operations on board the aircraft carrier *Graf Zeppelin*, which in the event was never completed. The carrier-based dive-bomber featured jettisonable landing gear, folding wings and an arrester hook. Those aircraft that had entered production were instead completed as land-based Ju 87B-2s.

In order to provide additional range, especially for anti-shipping operations, Junkers developed the Ju 87R (for *Reichweite*, or 'range'), as a derivative of the B-series. To compensate for the extra fuel, these aircraft were usually restricted to the carriage of a single 250kg (551lb) bomb.

Afrika Korps soldiers watch a flight of Stukas return from a mission. Stukas were used extensively in North Africa.

Junkers Ju 87B-1
Weight (Maximum take-off) 4250kg (9370lb)
Dimensions Length: 11m (36ft 1in), Wingspan: 13.8m (45ft 3in), Height: 3.77m (12ft 5in)
Powerplant One 882kW (1200hp) Junkers Jumo 211Da 12 cylinder engine
Speed 350km/h (217mph)
Range 600km (373 miles)
Ceiling 8100m (26,570ft)
Crew 2
Armament Two 7.92mm (0.31in) MG 17 machine guns (forward firing), one 7.92mm (0.31in) MG 15 machine gun (cockpit rear); 500kg (1102lb) bombload

GROUND-ATTACK AND RECONNAISSANCE AIRCRAFT

Junkers Ju 87B-2
This aircraft was part of I Gruppe, Stukageschwader 76, and flew in the France campaign in the summer of 1940.

Jumo Engine
In Ju 87B form the Stuka was powered by a 12-cylinder liquid-cooled Junkers Jumo 211Da engine. This was more powerful than the Jumo 210 in the A-series.

Undercarriage
Robust 'spatted' main undercarriage was a key feature of the Ju 87, although the fairings were often removed to cope with winter conditions on the Eastern Front.

Junkers Ju 87B-2
Weight (Maximum take-off) 4250kg (9370lb)
Dimensions Length: 11m (36ft 1in), Wingspan: 13.8m (45ft 3in), Height: 3.77m (12ft 5in)
Powerplant One 883kW (1200hp) Junkers Jumo 211Da 12 cylinder engine
Speed 350km/h (217mph)
Range 600km (373 miles)
Ceiling 8100m (26,570ft)
Crew 2
Armament Two 7.92mm (0.31in) MG 17 machine guns (forward firing), one 7.92mm (0.31in) MG 15 machine gun (cockpit rear); 1000kg (2205lb) bombload

GROUND-ATTACK AND RECONNAISSANCE AIRCRAFT

Tailplane
To provide additional strength, the Ju 87B's two-spar tailplane was braced by two external struts, replaced on the improved Ju 87D by single aerodynamic struts. The elevators were used in conjunction with aerodynamic brakes to help pull out of a dive.

Gull Wing
The very strong inverted gull wing was based on a two-spar structure with closely spaced ribs. The centre section was integral with the fuselage. Ailerons and flaps were provided.

GROUND-ATTACK AND RECONNAISSANCE AIRCRAFT

Junkers Ju 87R-2

3./Stukageschwader 5 flew this long-range Ju 87R-2, J9+LL, on the Eastern Front in March 1943. Based at Alakurtti near Murmansk, the aircraft received a winter coat of distemper.

Ju 87D series

The next major improvement to the Stuka line was the Ju 87D, which entered production as the Ju 87D-1 with a 1051kW (1410hp) Jumo 211J-1 engine and additional armour protection for the two-man crew. A strengthened version was the Ju 87D-2, intended for use as a glider tug, while the Ju 87D-3 was another ground-attack derivative, with yet further armour protection added. One extraordinary development of the Ju 87D-3 was a version with experimental personnel transport pods fitted on the upper surfaces of the wings. Each pod could accommodate two passengers and was designed to be released in a shallow dive, descending to the ground under a large parachute.

The Ju 87D-4 torpedo-bomber did not enter production, in contrast to the Ju 87D-5, which was a dedicated close-support aircraft with jettisonable landing gear and with the previous dive brakes deleted; the wingtips were meanwhile extended to counter the

Junkers Ju 87R-2

Another of the long-range Ju 87R-2s, this example from 6./Stukageschwader 2 'Immelmann' was based at Trimini, Libya, in 1941.

Junkers Ju 87R-2

Weight (Maximum take-off) 5100kg (11,240lb)
Dimensions Length: 11.50m (37ft 8in); Wingspan: 13.8m (45ft 3in); Height: 4.01m (13ft 2in)
Powerplant One 883kW (1200hp) Jumo 211Da in-line engine
Speed 410km/h (254mph)
Range 960km (593 miles)
Ceiling 7285m (23,900ft)
Crew 2
Armament Two 7.92mm (0.31in) MG 17 machine guns (forward firing), one 7.92mm (0.31in) MG 15 machine gun (cockpit rear); one 250kg (550lb) bomb; two 300 litre (79 US gal) drop tanks

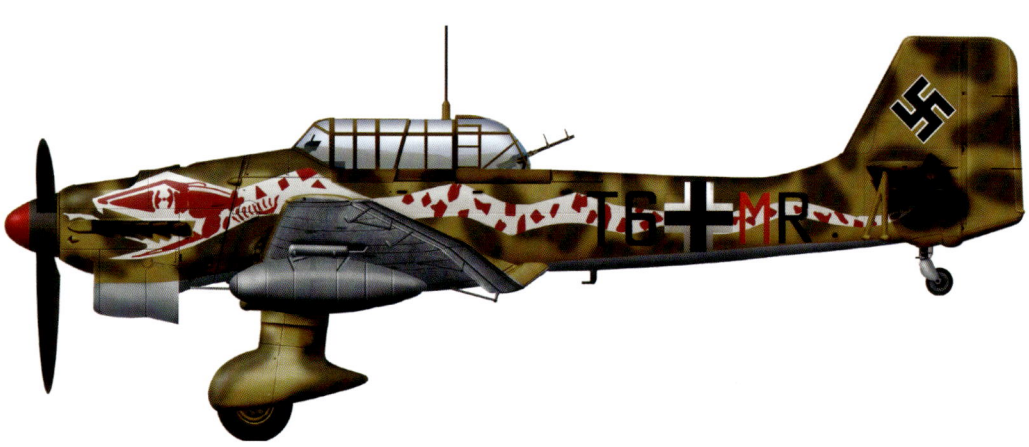

GROUND-ATTACK AND RECONNAISSANCE AIRCRAFT

Junkers Ju 87D-1

This Ju 87D-1 served with I./Stukageschwader 2 based in Russia in 1942.

Junkers Ju 87D-1
Weight (Maximum take-off) 6600kg (14,550lb)
Dimensions Length: 11.50m (37ft 8in), Wingspan: 13.8m (45ft 3in), Height: 3.88m (12ft 8in)
Powerplant One 1051kW (1410hp) Junkers Jumo 211J-1 engine
Speed 410km/h (255mph)
Range 1535km (950 miles)
Ceiling 7285m (23,900ft)
Crew 2
Armament Two 7.92mm (0.31in) MG 17 machine guns (forward firing), one 7.92mm (0.31in) MG 15 machine gun (cockpit rear); 1000kg (2205lb) bombload

increasing weight of the D-series. The Ju 87D-7 was another ground-attack model, but was tailored for night operations; converted from Ju 87D-3s and D-5s, these aircraft were powered by the 1119kW (1500hp) Jumo 211P and had their wing-mounted 7.92mm (0.31in) MG 17 machine guns replaced by 20mm (0.8in) MG 151/20 cannon. The defensive armament remained unchanged: a twin 7.92mm (0.31in) MG 81Z machine gun in the rear cockpit. Once adapted for daytime operations, the Ju 87D-7 became the Ju 87D-8, which had the night-flying gear – including flame-dampers – deleted.

Ju 87G series

There were plans to further refine the Stuka airframe to produce a Ju 87F version, which would also have featured a wing of increased span and a more powerful engine. Such were the changes eventually anticipated that the F-series was renamed as the Ju 187, but no production resulted.

Instead, the final operational version of the Stuka was the Ju 87G-1, a conversion of the Ju 87D-5 intended for the anti-armour role. Here, the armament was based around a single 37mm (1.45in) cannon under each wing. Other Ju 87Ds were adapted as dual-control trainers under the revised designation Ju 87H.

Combat record

The Ju 87 was outclassed during the Battle of Britain in 1940 – at the height of the battle, from 13–18 August 1940, Royal Air Force Hurricanes and Spitfires were credited with destroying no fewer than 41 Stukas, forcing the type's withdrawal from that campaign on 19 August 1940.

While the Ju 87 had proven itself as an attack asset, it was clear that it was unable to operate without interference from enemy fighters without taking heavy losses in the process. Despite this change in fortunes, the type continued to be widely used in the Mediterranean and Eastern Front theatres, where the definitive D-series had become available by early 1941.

In the Greek campaign, the Stuka was able to operate with little in the way of Allied air opposition and was particularly successful in attacking shipping – ultimately, the Ju 87 was credited with more ships sunk than any other aircraft in history.

At the start of Operation 'Barbarossa', the German attack on the Soviet Union that began on 22 June 1941, the elements of the Luftwaffe in theatre boasted eight Stuka *Gruppen*, possessing a total of 324 aircraft. Although employed widely in the opening months of the campaign, by 1943 losses were mounting and the type was switched mainly to night-time missions.

Nevertheless, for Operation 'Citadel', the major German offensive of July 1943, aimed at the central front near Kursk, the Luftwaffe was still able to call upon around 360 Stukas – mostly D-series aircraft, but also a small number of the recently received Ju 87Gs. The offensive commenced on 5 July, and in the days to follow dive-bomber crews flew up to six

GROUND-ATTACK AND RECONNAISSANCE AIRCRAFT

sorties per day. Bomb-carrying Stukas typically attacked targets in the Soviet rear areas, while 'Gustavs' attacked enemy tanks caught in the open. In autumn 1943 the *Stukageschwader* underwent a reorganization, emerging as *Schlachtgeschwader* ('ground-attack wings'). At the same time, the more survivable Focke-Wulf Fw 190F began to be drafted in to replace the Ju 87Ds, although each *Geschwader* typically retained a squadron of Ju 87Gs for anti-armour work.

Export Ju 87s were delivered to Bulgaria, Hungary, Italy and Romania and by the time production ended in September 1944 more than 5700 examples had been completed. Despite the type's obsolescence, no fewer than 125 Ju 87s were still officially on strength with the Luftwaffe when the war in Europe came to an end in April 1945.

Junkers Ju 87G-2
Weight (Maximum take-off) 3930kg (8664lb)
Dimensions Length: 11.50m (37ft 8in), Wingspan: 15m (49ft 2in), Height: 3.88m (12ft 8in)
Powerplant One 1044kW (1420hp) Junkers Jumo 210J-1 engine
Speed 380km/h (236mph)
Range 790km (490 miles)
Ceiling 8000m (26,240ft)
Crew 2
Armament Two 37mm (1.46in) Bordkanone 3,7; one 7.92mm (0.31in) MG 15 machine gun (cockpit)

Junkers Ju 87G-1
Bordkanone-toting Ju 87G-1 DJ+FT was assigned to a test unit active at the time of the Kursk offensive in July 1943.

Junkers Ju 87G-2
Flown by the leading exponent of the Stuka, Hans-Ulrich Rudel, this winter-camouflaged Ju 87G-2 was flying from Märkisch-Friedland in January 1945. The operating unit was the *Stab* flight of 10.(Panzerjäger)/Schlachtgeschwader 2.

Henschel Hs 126

The Henschel Hs 126 two-seat, short-range reconnaissance aircraft traces its lineage to the same company's parasol-winged Hs 122 that was developed in 1935 as a successor to the Heinkel He 45 and He 46, powered by a 492kW (660hp) Siemens SAM 22B engine.

Henschel Hs 126A-1

An Hs 126A-1 flown by 9.(Heeres-)/Lehrgeschwader 2, active from Chalons, Belgium, in June 1940.

Although a small number of these aircraft were completed, they did not enter frontline Luftwaffe service but instead served to inform chief designer Friedrich Nicolaus's subsequent Hs 126. The new aircraft employed an entirely revised wing, cantilever main undercarriage and a canopy over the pilot's cockpit (although the observer's position was left uncovered). The first prototype was based on a reworked Hs 122A airframe adapted for a 455kW (610hp) Junkers Jumo 210 engine and was first flown in autumn 1936. Another two developmental aircraft were completed, both now incorporating an 634kW (850hp) Bramo Fafnir 323A-1. Other changes included a redesigned rudder and the addition of bracing struts on the tailplane.

A total of 10 pre-production Hs 126A-0 aircraft were completed in 1937, these being essentially the same configuration as the third prototype. A number of the pre-production aircraft were used for evaluation by the Luftwaffe's *Lehrgeschwader* training unit in spring 1938. The initial-production Hs 126A-1 was generally similar to the A-0, but was powered by an 656kW (880hp) BMW 132Dc radial engine. Armament comprised a single forward-firing 7.92mm (0.31in) MG 17 machine gun plus a similar weapon on a trainable mount fired from the rear cockpit. Offensive stores consisted of five 10kg (22lb) bombs or a single 50kg (110lb) bomb on an under-fuselage rack. For reconnaissance work, a single Zeiss camera in a rear-fuselage bay was supplemented by a handheld camera in the rear cockpit.

Six of the A-1s were employed for combat trials in Spain in 1938 and, following use by the Condor Legion, were passed on to the Spanish Nationalist air arm, while 16 more examples were delivered to Greece. The Hellenic Air Force examples saw combat against Italian aircraft during the early stages of the Balkans campaign in April 1941.

Henschel Hs 126A-1
Weight (Maximum take-off) 3090kg (6820lb)
Dimensions Length: 10.9m (35ft 7in), Wingspan: 14.5m (47ft 7in), Height: 3.8m (12ft 4in)
Powerplant One 656kW (880hp) BMW 132Dc radial engine
Speed 356km/h (221mph)
Range 998 km (620 miles)
Ceiling 8530m (28,000ft)
Crew 2
Armament Two 7.92mm (0.31in) MG 17 machine guns (one forward firing, one in rear of cockpit); five 10kg (22lb) bombs, or one 50kg (110lb) bomb

The improved Hs 126B-1 arrived in service in summer 1939 with additional radio equipment and either the 634kW (850hp) Bramo 323A-1 or 671kW (900hp) Bramo 323A-2 engine.

Operational service

Production aircraft were completed at Schönefeld and Johannisthal in Berlin. The initial Hs 126A-1 aircraft entered operational service with Aufklärungsgruppe 35 and by the outbreak of the war the replacement of He 45 and He 46 aircraft within the Luftwaffe's reconnaissance units was well under way.

GROUND-ATTACK AND RECONNAISSANCE AIRCRAFT

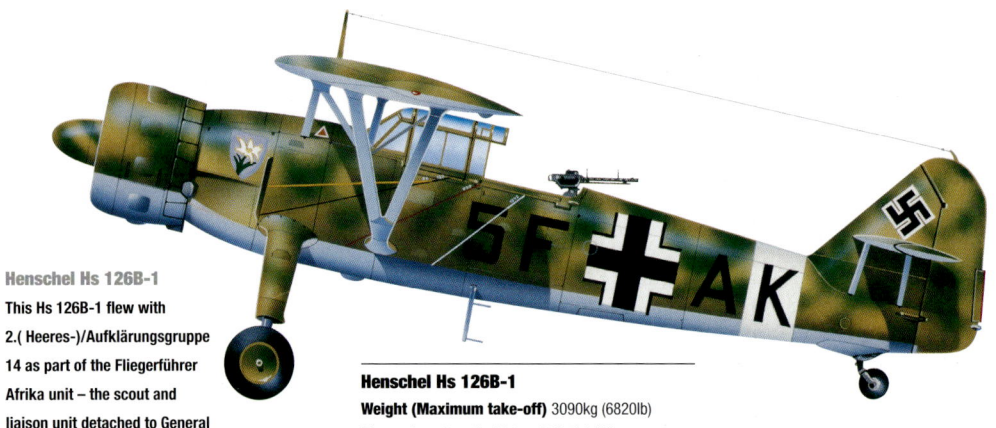

Henschel Hs 126B-1

This Hs 126B-1 flew with 2.(Heeres-)/Aufklärungsgruppe 14 as part of the Fliegerführer Afrika unit – the scout and liaison unit detached to General Rommel's HQ – during July 1941.

At the beginning of World War II, Hs 126s equipped some 80 per cent of German battlefield reconnaissance units. A notable secondary mission was glider towing, and it was Hs 126s that were used to tow 10 DFS 230 gliders on the Gran Sasso raid to rescue Benito Mussolini on 12 September 1943.

Henschel Hs 126B-1
Weight (Maximum take-off) 3090kg (6820lb)
Dimensions Length: 10.9m (35ft 7in), Wingspan: 14.5m (47ft 7in), Height: 3.8m (12ft 4in)
Powerplant One 671kW (900hp) Bramo 323A-2 engine
Speed 356km/h (221mph)
Range 998 km (620 miles)
Ceiling 8530m (28,000ft)
Crew 2
Armament Two 7.92mm (0.31in) MG 17 machine guns; five 10kg (22lb) bombs, or one 50kg (110lb) bomb

A total of over 600 Hs 126s were eventually built, but from 1942 the type began to be withdrawn from frontline service in favour of the Focke-Wulf Fw 189. Ironically, the early development of the latter type had been stalled by the Luftwaffe's unwillingness to give up the Hs 126A-1 and B-1, the high command initially refusing to replace them despite their growing obsolescence.

Fieseler Fi 156 *Storch*

A two- or three-seat army cooperation/reconnaissance aircraft, the Fi 156 *Storch* ('stork') is now the best-remembered Fieseler design of the war.

Widely used by the Luftwaffe throughout the conflict, the Fieseler Fi 156 set the trend for subsequent aircraft in its class, with a combination of excellent short take-off and landing (STOL) performance and an extensively glazed cockpit, giving the crew useful downwards visibility.

First flight

The product of Gerhard Fieseler and his chief designer Reinhold Mewes, the Fi 156 was first flown in early 1936 and was a braced high-wing monoplane employing mixed construction. The tail unit was of the conventional, braced type, while the undercarriage comprised long-stroke main units and a fixed tail-skid. Power was provided by a single Argus inverted-Vee air-cooled piston engine.

The aircraft's STOL capability was the result of a wing equipped with high-lift devices, including – in the initial production series – a fixed slat that extended over the full span of the leading edge, while the trailing edge was equipped with slotted ailerons and, across its full length, slotted camber-changing flaps.

The first three prototypes (Fi 156 V1, V2 and V3) demonstrated the ability to take off over a distance of around 60 metres (200ft) with only a light breeze. Little more than a third of this distance was required for landing.

Test models

The initial three prototypes were followed by the ski-equipped Fi 156 V4 and were tested in competition with rival designs from Messerschmitt and Schiebel, as well as an autogyro designed by Focke-Wulf. After the pre-production Fi 156 V5, a total of 10 pre-production Fi 156A-0 aircraft were completed for service evaluation in early 1937.

GROUND-ATTACK AND RECONNAISSANCE AIRCRAFT

In July the same year one of the pre-production machines was demonstrated for the first time in public, by which time the aircraft was in series production as the Fi 156A-1. Prior to World War II, the *Storch* was used mainly for staff transport work on behalf of the Luftwaffe, but a small number of Fi 156A-1s did see early combat action when they were deployed to Spain for battlefield observation in 1937. After two early losses to Republican fighters, the aircraft were relegated to communications work behind Nationalist lines. A planned Fi 156B variant with movable leading-edge

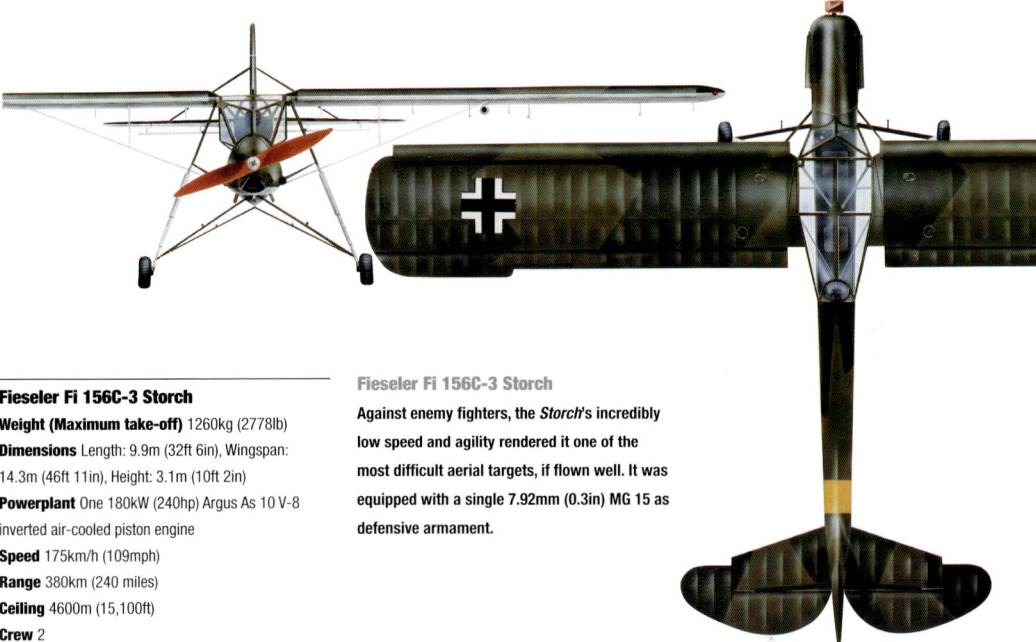

Fieseler Fi 156C-3 Storch
Weight (Maximum take-off) 1260kg (2778lb)
Dimensions Length: 9.9m (32ft 6in), Wingspan: 14.3m (46ft 11in), Height: 3.1m (10ft 2in)
Powerplant One 180kW (240hp) Argus As 10 V-8 inverted air-cooled piston engine
Speed 175km/h (109mph)
Range 380km (240 miles)
Ceiling 4600m (15,100ft)
Crew 2
Armament One 7.92mm (0.31in) MG 15 machine gun

Fieseler Fi 156C-3 Storch

Against enemy fighters, the *Storch*'s incredibly low speed and agility rendered it one of the most difficult aerial targets, if flown well. It was equipped with a single 7.92mm (0.3in) MG 15 as defensive armament.

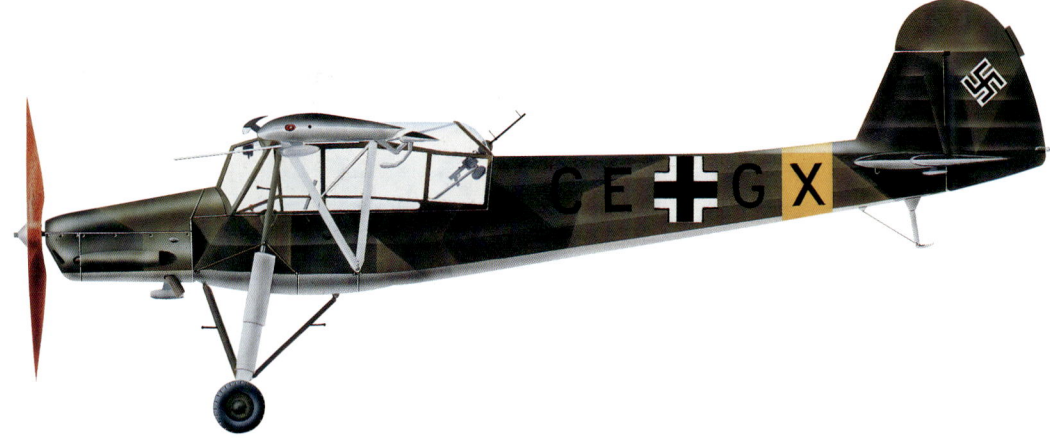

slats was not built, and the next major production variant was the C-series.

156C series

The pre-production Fi 156C-0 was an improved Fi 156A-1 with raised glazing over the rear of the cabin to permit installation of a defensive 7.92mm (0.31in) machine gun – reflecting lessons learned during service in the Spanish Civil War. The aircraft entered quantity production as the Fi 156C-1 equipped as a liaison and staff transport, and the Fi 156C-2, which was a reconnaissance variant with a single camera and two-man crew. Other C-2s were outfitted for casualty evacuation, with provision for a single stretcher patient.

The Fi 156C-3 was intended for general-purpose use and some of these aircraft introduced an improved Argus As 10P engine in place of the previous As 10C. When equipped for desert operations this became the Fi 156C-3/Trop with engine filters to protect against dust and sand.

With the As 10P engine incorporated as standard, the aircraft was re-designated as the Fi 156C-5, which also had provision for a single drop tank below the fuselage (increasing the aircraft's range by almost a factor of three) or a camera installation; it, too, was tropicalized as the Fi 156C-5/Trop.

In order to provide an improved air ambulance, Fieseler developed the Fi 156D-0 pre-production aircraft with improved accommodation for a single stretcher via an enlarged loading/unloading hatch, but with the earlier Argus As 10C powerplant. This was launched into production as the Fi 156D-1 that now featured the As 10P engine as standard.

Tracked landing gear was trialled on a pre-production batch of Fi 156E-0 aircraft, but only these 10 E-series aircraft were ever built.

Famous exploits

Total production of all variants amounted to almost 2900 aircraft. Its wartime exploits in the hands of the Luftwaffe included the rescue of Italian leader Benito Mussolini from his imprisonment in a hotel high in the Apennine Mountains on 12 September 1943. Meanwhile, test pilot Hanna Reitsch flew into the ruins of Berlin on 26 April 1945 carrying General Ritter von Greim, who Hitler would appoint as the new – and final – commander of the Nazi-era Luftwaffe.

As well as production in Germany, wartime Fi 156s rolled out of factories in France (where they were produced by Morane-Saulnier), and Czechoslovakia (Mraz). Both companies continued production after the war as the M.S.500 series and the K-65 Cáp, respectively, and a single example was also built, unlicensed, by Antonov in the Soviet Union as the OKA-38.

Fieseler Fi 156C-5

Weight (Maximum take-off) 1260kg (2778lb)
Dimensions Length: 9.9m (32ft 6in), Wingspan: 14.3m (46ft 11in), Height: 3.1m (10ft 2in)
Powerplant One 199kW (270hp) Argus As 10P V-8 inverted-V air-cooled piston engine
Speed 175km/h (109mph)
Range 380km (240 miles)
Ceiling 4600m (15,100ft)
Crew 2
Armament One 7.92mm (0.31in) MG 15 machine gun

Fieseler Fi 156C-5

This Fi 156C-5 was operated by 1.(Heeres-)/Aufklärungsgruppe 32, active in Finland in January 1941. Coincidentally, the *Staffel* emblem was a stork – painted here on the nose.

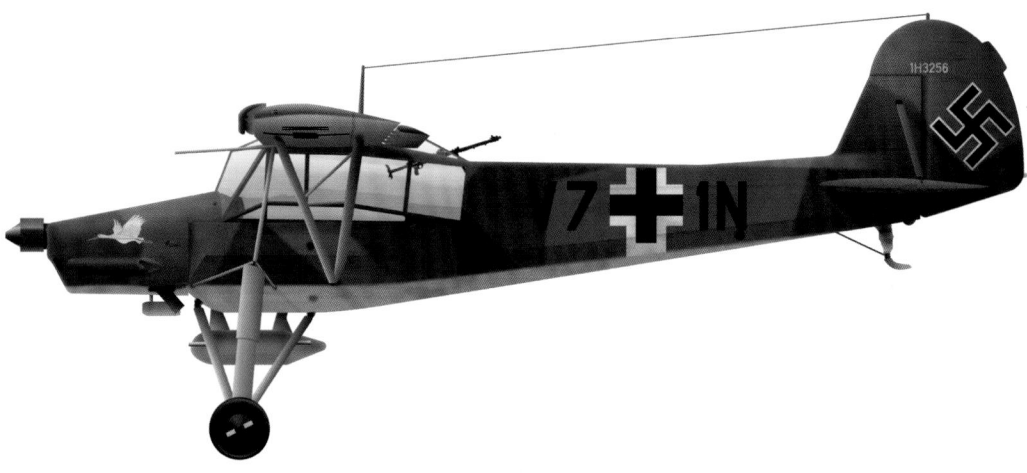

Fock-Wulf Fw 189 *Uhu*

The Fw 189 *Uhu* ('eagle owl') was one of several designs produced in response to a *Reichsluftfahrtministerium* (German Air Ministry) requirement of February 1937 calling for a short-range reconnaissance aircraft.

Alongside offerings from Arado and Hamburger Flugzeugbau, Focke-Wulf's Kurt Tank created an all-metal, stressed-skin, low-wing monoplane with an extensively glazed fuselage pod between twin booms carrying the tail surfaces. The main wheels retracted to the rear, to be accommodated within the booms. The crew nacelle had accommodation for the pilot, navigator/radio operator and engineer/gunner, and the first prototype, Fw 187 V1, was powered by a pair of 321kW (430hp) Argus As 410 engines. Construction of the initial prototype began in April 1937 and it was first flown by Tank himself in July 1938.

The second prototype, Fw 187 V2, flown in August 1938, added armament in the form of a single 7.92mm (0.31in) MG 15 machine gun in each of the nose, dorsal and rear positions, as well as two fixed MG 17 machine guns of the same calibre in the wing roots. Four underwing racks could each carry a single 50kg (110lb) bomb. A third prototype, Fw 187 V3, took to the air in September 1938, this time with Argus air-pressure-actuated, variable-pitch propellers.

The fourth prototype took to the air after Focke-Wulf had received a development contract for the production Fw 189A, powered by As 410A-1 engines and with armament of just two MG 15s. A pre-production batch of 10 Fw 189A-0 aircraft to the same standard as the fourth prototype were built at Bremen in 1940 and some were issued to the 9.(H)/Lehrgeschwader 2 for operational trials. The initial-production Fw 189A-1 retained the single flexible MG 15s in dorsal and rear positions but reinstated the wing-root MG 17s and bomb racks. Subvariants were the Fw 189A-1/Trop with desert survival equipment and the Fw 189A-1/U2 and U3 VIP transports.

Prototype forerunner
The ninth prototype was the forerunner of the subsequent Fw 189A-2 variant, introduced in late 1942, and with the flexible MG 15s replaced by twin 7.92mm (0.31in) MG 81Zs. A two-seat dual-control trainer, the Fw 189A-3, was produced in only limited quantities, while the fifth prototype tested more significant modifications for the training role: it was followed by the productionized Fw 189B with a redesigned fuselage nacelle, a stepped cockpit and reduced glazing. B-series production accounted for three pre-

Focke-Wulf Fw 189A-1 Uhu
Pressed into service as a night fighter, this aircraft – fitted with the *Schräge Musik* ('jazz music') upward-firing cannon angled at 60–70 degrees from the horizontal – flew from Greifswald in February 1945. The aircraft also includes FuG 212 AI radar in the nose.

Focke-Wulf Fw 189A-1 Uhu
Weight (Maximum take-off) 3950kg (8708lb)
Dimensions Length: 11.9m (39ft 1in), Wingspan: 18.4m (60ft 4in), Height: 3.1m (10ft 2in)
Powerplant Two 342kW (459hp) Argus As 410A-1 V-12 inverted-V air-cooled piston engines
Speed 344km/h (214mph)
Range 940 km (580 miles)
Ceiling 7000m (23,000ft)
Crew 3
Armament Two flexible 7.92mm (0.31in) MG 15 machine guns (dorsal and rear positions), two fixed 7.92mm (0.31in) MG 17 machine guns (wing roots), plus one *Schräge Musik* upward-firing 20mm (0.8in) MG FF autocannon

series Fw 189B-0 aircraft and 10 Fw 189B-1 five-seat crew trainers; some of these entered service in advance of the A-series, joining the 9.(H)/LG 2 training unit in the spring and summer of 1940.

A-series

Meanwhile, development of the A-series continued, including the Fw 189A-4 in late 1942. This was a light ground-attack aircraft with 20mm (0.8in) MG 151/20 cannon in the wing roots, plus armour protection in the underside of the fuselage and for the engines and fuel tanks. A more extensive rework was envisaged for the close-support Fw 189C, based on the modified first (Fw 189 V1b) and the sixth prototype. It replaced the crew nacelle with a much smaller two-man cockpit and was heavily armoured; it was abandoned in favour of the rival Henschel Hs 129.

The seventh prototype was expected to begin life as a trials aircraft for the proposed Fw 189D twin-float trainer, but in the event was completed as an Fw 189B-0. Another proposed version was the Fw 189E, which would have been built by SNCASO in France with a revised powerplant of two 522kW (700hp) Gnome-Rhône 14M radial engines. At least one example was built on the basis of an Fw 189A-4, but it crashed during its ferry flight to Germany, where it was to be evaluated. Other examples of the *Uhu* were manufactured by Aero in Prague.

Everything about the Fw 189 was slender, especially the wings and tail booms. Despite this, it was an immensely strong aircraft and able to absorb large amounts of battle damage.

GROUND-ATTACK AND RECONNAISSANCE AIRCRAFT

Focke-Wulf Fw 189A-1 Uhu
Nachtkette/NAGr. 15 (Night Reconnaissance Group 15) flew nocturnal reconnaissance sorties for the Fourth *Panzerarmee* in southern Poland in 1944. The unit was based at an airfield near Naglowitz.

The final production versions from a manufacturing run of 864 aircraft were the F-series. The Fw 189F-1 was broadly similar to the Fw 189A-2, but was re-engined with 433kW (580hp) Argus As 411MA-1 powerplants; while the Fw 189F-2 featured the same engines, but introduced electrically-operated landing gear, increased fuel capacity and more armour protection.

Henschel Hs 129

The Hs 129 was intended to meet a German Air Ministry requirement for a twin-engine ground-attack aircraft armed with at least one 20mm (0.8in) cannon and with extensive armour protection.

The prototype Hs 129 first flew in spring 1939 and was characterized by a triangular-section fuselage that offered limited space for the cockpit – accommodation was notably cramped, but the single pilot was provided with a windscreen of 75mm (2.95in) armoured glass, while the nose itself was constructed of armour plating. A total of three prototypes underwent Luftwaffe evaluation, each being powered by a pair of 347kW (465hp) Argus As 410 engines. In this original form, the cockpit arrangement was judged unacceptable and the aircraft's performance was generally poor.

Production variant
Another eight Hs 129A-0 pre-production aircraft were completed for further test and evaluation, but the proposed Hs 129A-1 initial-production variant was abandoned in favour of the Hs 129B-1. This featured a number of improvements, including more powerful 522kW (700hp) Gnome-Rhône 14M 4/5 radial engines that had been trialled in the 10 pre-series Hs 129B-0 aircraft, delivered for evaluation from December 1941.

The Hs 129B-1 version entered service with 4./Schlachtgeschwader 1 in April 1942 and thereafter saw extensive use on the Eastern Front. Other Hs 129s saw combat in North Africa, Italy and in France after the D-Day landings. Subvariants of the B-1 included the Hs 129B-1/R1 with provision for two 50kg (110lb) bombs or 96 anti-personnel bomblets and the Hs 129B-1/R2 armed with a 30mm (1.18in) MK 101 cannon under the fuselage. Meanwhile, the Hs 129B-1/R3 was armed with four additional 7.92mm (0.31in) MG 17 machine guns and the Hs 129B-1/R4 replaced the R1's bombs with a single 250kg (551lb) weapon. Finally, the Hs 129B-1/R5 was equipped for reconnaissance with a single camera.

Improved Hs 129B-2
Early 1943 saw the arrival of the improved Hs 129B-2 series, starting with the Hs 129B-2/R1 with heavier weapons for anti-tank work: initially, two 20mm (0.8in) MG 151/20 cannons and two 13mm (0.51in) MG 131 machine guns. The similar Hs 129B-2/R2 had an additional 30mm (1.18in)

GROUND-ATTACK AND RECONNAISSANCE AIRCRAFT

MK 103 cannon under the fuselage, replaced on the Hs 129B-2/R3 by a 37mm (1.45in) BK 3,7 and with the MG 131s deleted. Harder-hitting still was the Hs 129B-2/R4 with a 75mm (2.96in) PaK 40 gun in a pod below the fuselage and the Hs 129B-2/R3 that was similar, but with an electro-pneumatically operated 75mm (2.96in) BK 7,5 gun in place of the PaK 40. A measure of the power of these larger-calibre weapons is seen in the fact that even the 30mm (1.18in) MK 101 cannon had a lethal effect against all armoured vehicles except main battle tanks, and that even these were sometimes vulnerable when attacked from the rear.

Meanwhile, the huge 75mm (2.96in) PaK 40 anti-tank gun was able to penetrate 133mm (5.25in) of armour at a range of 1000m (3280ft) if the shell hit square-on. While a single good hit was usually sufficient to destroy a tank, even from head-on, and the cyclic rate of fire of 40 rounds per minute was impressive, the gun itself was simply too powerful for the aircraft, resulting in seriously compromised performance. Hs 129 production eventually totalled 879 aircraft, including prototypes.

Henschel Hs 129B-3
Weight (Maximum take-off) 5250kg (11,574lb)
Dimensions Length: 9.75m (32ft), Wingspan: 14.2m (46ft 7in), Height: 3.25m (10ft 8in)
Powerplant Two 522kW (700hp) Gnome-Rhône 14M 4/5 radial engines
Speed 407km/h (253mph)
Range 690km (430 miles)
Ceiling 9000m (30,000ft)
Crew 1
Armament One 75mm (2.96in) BK 7,5 (Bordkanone 7,5)

Henschel Hs 129B-1
8./Schlachtgeschwader 1's fleet included this Hs 129B-1, based at El Aluin, Tunisia, in February 1943.

Henschel Hs 129B-1
Weight (Maximum take-off) 5250kg (11,574lb)
Dimensions Length: 9.75m (32ft), Wingspan: 14.2m (46ft 7in), Height: 3.25m (10ft 8in)
Powerplant Two 522kW (700hp) Gnome-Rhône 14M 4/5 radial engines
Speed 407km/h (253mph)
Range 690km (430 miles)
Ceiling 9000m (30,000ft)
Crew 1
Armament Two 20mm (0.8in) cannon, two 7.92mm (0.31in) MG machine guns; up to 250kg (551lb) bombload

Henschel Hs 129B-3
This Hs 129B-3 was flown by 14.(Panzerjäger)/Schlachtgeschwader 9, one of only two operational units to fly the B-3 with the BK 7,5 cannon carried in a jettisonable fairing.

Henschel Hs 132

Although destined never to see service with the Luftwaffe, the Hs 132 was a remarkable attempt to develop a jet-powered dive-bomber that would have provided such speed in the dive that it would have been all but immune to attack from ground defences.

The single-seat aircraft was intended to reach a terminal velocity of more than 805km/h (500mph) and as a result the designers created a prone position for the pilot, which allowed him to sustain loadings of up to 12g.

A computerized bombsight would have been used to aid the pilot in 'tossing' the bomb at the target before climbing back out of range of anti-aircraft fire.

Specification

The Hs 132A was to be powered by a 800kg (1764lb) thrust BMW 003A-1 turbojet in a nacelle mounted above the fuselage. There were also plans for an Hs 132B with a 900kg (1984lb) thrust Jumo 004B-2 engine and the Hs 132C with a 1300kg (2866lb) thrust Heinkel-Hirth 011A-1.

While the initial A-model was to have been armed with only a single 500kg (1102lb) bomb, the Hs 132B would have added a pair of 20mm (0.8in) MG 151 cannon and six or eight anti-tank rockets.

Finally, the Hs 132C would have retained the 500kg (1102lb) bomb and twin 20mm (0.8in) weapons but would have also added a pair of 30mm (1.18in) MK 103 cannon. A planned Hs 132D would have introduced a new wing of increased span.

Prototypes incomplete

Construction of three prototypes was begun in March 1945, but only the prototype for the Hs 132A had been completed but not test flown when the factory was overrun by the Red Army.

Henschel Hs 132 V1

Henschel Hs 132 V1 ready for initial trials, spring 1945. The Soviet army occupied the factory before the aircraft could undergo test flights.

Henschel Hs 132A
Weight (Maximum take-off) 3400kg (7496lb)
Dimensions Length: 8.9m (29ft 2in), Wingspan: 7.2m (23ft 7in)
Powerplant One 7.8kN (1760lbf) thrust BMW 109-003E-2 turbojet engine
Speed 780km/h (480mph)
Range 680km (420 miles)
Ceiling 10,250m (33,630ft)
Crew 1
Armament One 500kg (1100lb) SD 500 bomb semi-recessed under the fuselage

GROUND-ATTACK AND RECONNAISSANCE AIRCRAFT

Blohm und Voss BV 141

The radically unorthodox BV 141 was the product of a 1937 specification issued by the *Reichsluftfahrtministerium* (RLM, German Air Ministry) calling for a single-engine, three-seat, short-range reconnaissance and observation aircraft.

The requirement placed particular emphasis on good all-round visibility. Responses were provided by Arado and Focke-Wulf, while Richard Vogt of the Hamburger Flugzeugbau GmbH offered a more novel approach to the requirement, with the BV 141 featuring an asymmetric layout based around an 645kW (865hp) BMW 132N radial engine installed in the forward end of a port-side tail boom and an extensively glazed crew nacelle mounted to starboard.

Prototypes

Despite the Focke-Wulf Fw 189 design finding official favour, Hamburger Flugzeugbau persisted with its design and continued work on the project as a private-venture initiative. A first prototype, the Ha 141-0 (initially with the civil registration D-ORJE, later designated as the BV 141 V2), took to the air on 25 February 1938.

Another two prototypes (BV 141 V1 and V3) followed it into the air in autumn of the same year, both being slightly larger than the initial aircraft and equipped with an entirely redesigned crew nacelle.

The third prototype was equipped with new, wide-track undercarriage and featured the proposed armament: two fixed forward-firing 7.92mm (0.31in) MG 17 machine guns, plus two MG 15 machine guns of the same calibre firing to the rear. The aircraft was also equipped to carry a camera and racks for four 50kg (110lb) bombs.

The third prototype showed enough potential during its initial trials for the company to receive an RLM order for five examples of the pre-production BV 141A. These had their wingspan increased to 15.45m (50ft 8in) and wing area increased to 42.86m² (461 sq ft) and they were each powered

Blohm und Voss BV 141B-0
This is the fourth BV 141B-0 pre-production aircraft (BV 141 V12), as seen when it was delivered to Tarnewitz for armament trials.

Blohm und Voss BV 141B-0
Weight (Maximum take-off) 6100kg (14,448lb)
Dimensions Length: 13.95m (45ft 9in), Wingspan: 17.4m (57ft 3in), Height: 3.6m (11ft 10in)
Powerplant One 1163kW (1560hp) BMW 801A radial engine
Speed 370km/h (230mph)
Range 1200km (746 miles)
Ceiling 9998m (32,801ft)
Crew 3
Armament Two 7.92mm (0.31in) MG 17 machine guns (fixed forward-firing), two 7.92mm (0.31in) MG 15 machine guns (rear cockpit); four 50kg (110lb) bombs

GROUND-ATTACK AND RECONNAISSANCE AIRCRAFT

by a single BMW Bramo 323 radial producing 746kW (1000hp).

Trials

The five BV 141A-0 aircraft (BV 141A-01/V4 to BV 141A-05/V8) underwent evaluation at Rechlin in late 1939 where they completed trials successfully, but plans for production were shelved in April 1940 since it was deemed the Bramo 323 engine lacked the power required.

Another five examples of the re-engined BV 141B-0 were ordered (BV 141B-01/V9 to BV 141B-10/V18), now fitted with the 1163kW (1560hp) BMW 801A radial engine, and the second of these aircraft undertook service trials with the Luftwaffe's Aufklärungsschule 1 reconnaissance training unit in autumn 1941.

New airframe

The B-series also featured an extensively redesigned and strengthened airframe. Externally, it could be distinguished by the equal taper introduced on its outer wing panels and asymmetric horizontal tail surfaces to improve the field of fire from the rear gun position in the glazed nacelle cone.

Despite these improvements, the BV 141 continued to suffer from delays – particularly related to deficiencies in the aircraft's hydraulic system – and the programme was finally abandoned altogether in 1943. By this stage its chances of success had been greatly reduced by the fact the rival Fw 189 was already in quantity production, while the chosen BMW 801 was in great demand for the Fw 190 production effort.

Blohm und Voss BV 141B-1
Weight (Maximum take-off) 5700kg (12,566lb)
Dimensions Length: 13.95m (45ft 9in), Wingspan: 7.4m (57ft 3in), Height: 3.6m (11ft 10in)
Powerplant One 1163kW (1560hp) BMW 801A radial engine
Speed 438km/h (272mph)
Range 1900km (1181 miles)
Ceiling 10,000m (32,808ft)
Crew 3
Armament Two 7.92mm (0.31in) MG 17 machine guns (fixed forward-firing), two 7.92mm (0.31in) MG 15 machine guns (rear cockpit); four 50kg (110lb) bombs

Blohm und Voss BV 141B-1
This aircraft was found abandoned at the Blohm und Voss works at Wenzendorf in 1945. The finish appears to be overall RLM02 *grau-grün* (grey-green) with standard mid-war markings. This machine may have been used for operational trials, since it carries a code that is out of sequence with those allocated to the other BV 141 prototypes.

TRANSPORTS AND GLIDERS

Before World War II, transport aircraft had been used only as troop carriers. But with the Luftwaffe a new role awaited them – that of air-landing operations in which soldiers were disembarked directly under fire on to enemy territory. The Junkers Ju 52/3m remained the most important Luftwaffe transport of the war, including carrying paratroopers into action for their famed attacks in the Low Countries, Scandinavia and Crete.

This chapter includes the following aircraft:

- Junkers Ju 52
- DFS 230
- Junkers Ju 290
- Arado Ar 232
- Messerschmitt Me 323 *Gigant*
- Siebel Si 204

The Junkers Ju-52 was used in every conceivable support and supply function, including transporting wounded *Gebirgsjäger* (mountain troops) and *Fallschirmjäger* (paratroopers), as seen here.

TRANSPORTS AND GLIDERS

Junkers Ju 52

The Luftwaffe's most famous transport traces its origins back to the decision to evaluate the single-engine Ju 52 commercial freight transport as a three-engine aircraft.

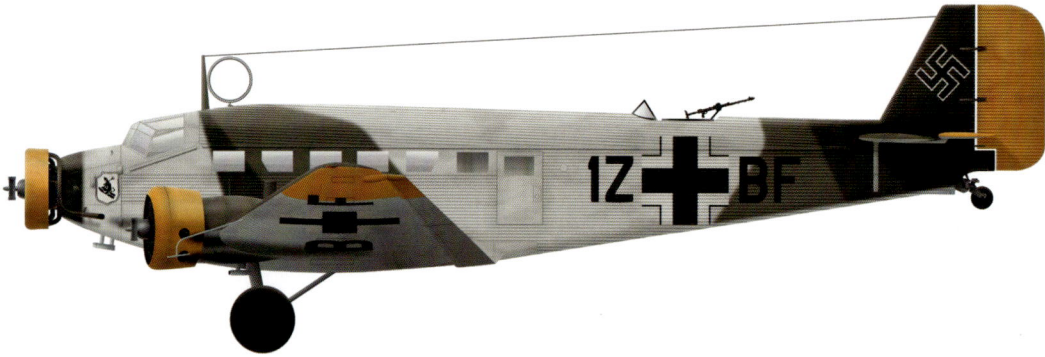

Only six examples of the original Ju 52 were completed and the first of these took to the air on 13 October 1930. The resulting Ju 52/3m prototype was created by adapting the seventh, unfinished, airframe on the Ju 52 production line. The original powerplant consisted of three 410kW (550hp) Pratt & Whitney Hornet engines, and this Ju 52/3mce variant began flight testing in April 1931.

Immediately, the aircraft demonstrated performance that far outstripped its single-engine forebearer. The new aircraft was ordered into production, the original Ju 52 production was terminated, and the first of the new trimotors were delivered to the launch customer Lloyd Aéreo Boliviano, which took seven aircraft beginning in 1932.

Initial Ju 52/3m production included aircraft with wheeled, float or ski landing gear, and while the aircraft delivered to Finland's Aero O/Y and Sweden's AB Aerotransport were provided with floats, those received by Deutsche Luft Hansa had wheeled undercarriage. By the end of 1935, production had reached 97 examples for airline use, of which 51 were flying with Lufthansa.

First combat

The trimotor was of interest to the clandestine Luftwaffe and an interim bomber version was created as the Ju 52/3mge, followed by the improved Ju 52/3mg3e, which was powered by three 541kW (725hp) BMW 123-A3 engines and which featured an upgraded radio and bomb-release mechanism. These aircraft underwent combat trials during the Spanish Civil War, where they initially flew as troop transports, including ferrying around 10,000 nationalist troops from Morocco to Spain. By the time the conflict ended in 1939, Ju 52/3m aircraft had flown 13,000 operational hours and dropped more than 6000 tonnes of bombs.

Deliveries to the Luftwaffe included 450 during 1934–35. While production of the civilian version continued, more than 230 were fielded by Luft-Hansa

Junkers Ju 52/3mg4e

Ju 52/3mg4e 1Z+BF was assigned to the *Stabsschwarm* (Staff Flight) of IV./Kampfgruppe zur besonderen Verwendung 1, taking part in assault operations over Crete in spring 1941.

Junkers Ju 52/3mg4e

Weight (Maximum take-off) 10,499kg (23,146lb)
Dimensions Length: 19.90m (62ft), Wingspan: 29.20m (95ft 10in), Height: 4.52m (14ft 10in)
Powerplant Three 541kW (725hp) BMW 132A-3 nine-cylinder radial engines
Speed 286km/h (178mph)
Range 1305km (811 miles)
Ceiling 5900m (19,360ft)
Crew 2/3, 17 passengers
Armament One 7.92mm (0.31in) MG 15 machine gun or 13mm (0.51in) MG 131 machine gun (dorsal)

from the mid-1930s. Production ramped up as Europe moved closer to war, and in 1939 the output reached 593 aircraft for the Luftwaffe alone. When World War II broke out, the military commandeered another 59 examples from Lufthansa.

The improved Ju 52/3mg4e was a military version that replaced the original tail-skid with a tailwheel and featured some internal equipment changes compared with the Ju 52/3mg3e. It was followed by the Ju 52/3mg5e, powered by three 619kW (830hp) BMW 132T engines and which used exhaust efflux for de-icing. It could operate with interchangeable wheel, float or ski landing gear and featured improved radio. The Ju 52/3mg6e was basically similar, but was simplified and available with wheeled undercarriage only; the radio was also simplified.

Next was the Ju 52/3mg7e, which was essentially similar to the 3mg6e but with autopilot and a large loading hatch. An additional hatch, this time in the roof, produced the Ju 52/3mg8e, the later examples of which were powered by more powerful BMW 132Z piston engines.

The Ju 52/3mg9e was similar to the late-production Ju 52/3mg8e, but had strengthened landing gear and was fitted with glider towing gear as standard. The Ju 52/3mg10e was also similar, but once again capable of either wheeled or float operations.

The next major version was the Ju 52/3mg12e; it was similar to the Ju 52/3mg10e but with three BMW 132L engines, and was also supplied to Lufthansa as the civilian Ju 52/3m12. The final production version was the Ju 52/3mg14e that featured additional armour protection for the pilot as well as increased defensive armament.

Wherever the Luftwaffe was at war, the Ju 53/3m found itself in action and proved to be an exceptionally versatile design. Demand was so great that additional production lines were

This photograph shows a Junkers Ju 52/3m at a forward airfield somewhere on the Eastern Front during early 1943. In this theatre, the Ju 52 was mainly tasked with resupplying troops.

TRANSPORTS AND GLIDERS

Junkers Ju 52/3mg5e
This Ju 52 served with I Gruppe, Kampfgeschwader zbV (Transport Wing) 172 in Italy, 1943.

Corrugation
The Ju 52/3m was an all-metal aircraft, covered mainly with corrugated Duralumin skinning. The corrugation gave the aircraft immense strength while keeping the weight of the aircraft low.

Cockpit
A crew of three flew the Ju 52, with a pilot and co-pilot sitting side-by-side and a radio operator sitting on a jump seat between them.

TRANSPORTS AND GLIDERS

Dorsal Armament
The dorsal hatch mounted a 7.92mm (0.31in) MG 15 machine gun. A transparent fairing was fixed in front of it to give the gunner some protection from the slipstream in flight.

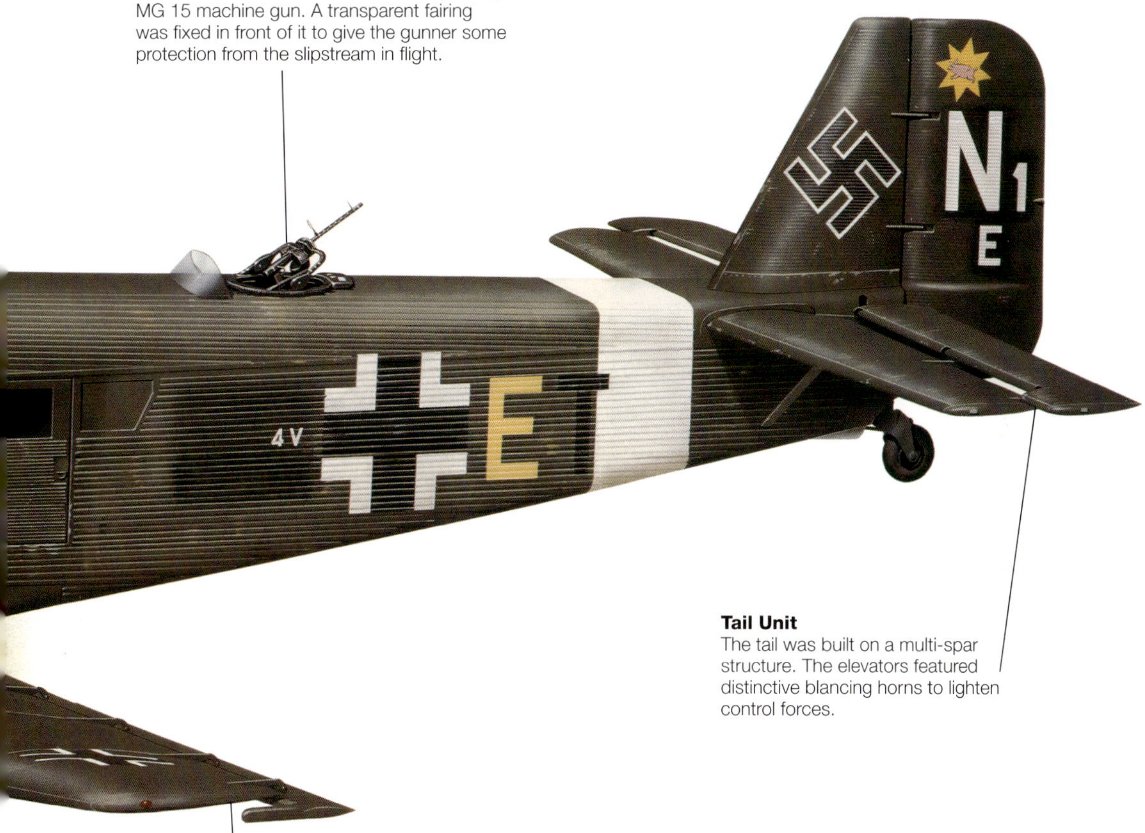

Tail Unit
The tail was built on a multi-spar structure. The elevators featured distinctive blancing horns to lighten control forces.

Wings
The Ju 52 featured a detached flap/aileron assembly, positioned below and behind the main wing structure. The ailerons dropped at low speed to act as partial flaps, which, together with the inboard slotted flaps, gave the aircraft great STOL cabability.

Junkers Ju 52/3mg5e

Weight (Maximum take-off) 11,030kg (24,317lb)
Dimensions Length: 19.90m (62ft), Wingspan: 29.20m (95ft 10in), Height: 4.52m (14ft 10in)
Powerplant Three 619kW (830hp) BMW 132T-2 nine-cylinder radial engines
Speed 286km/h (178mph)
Range 1305km (811 miles)
Ceiling 5900m (19,360ft)
Crew 2/3, 17 passengers
Armament One 7.92mm (0.31in) MG 15 machine gun (dorsal)

TRANSPORTS AND GLIDERS

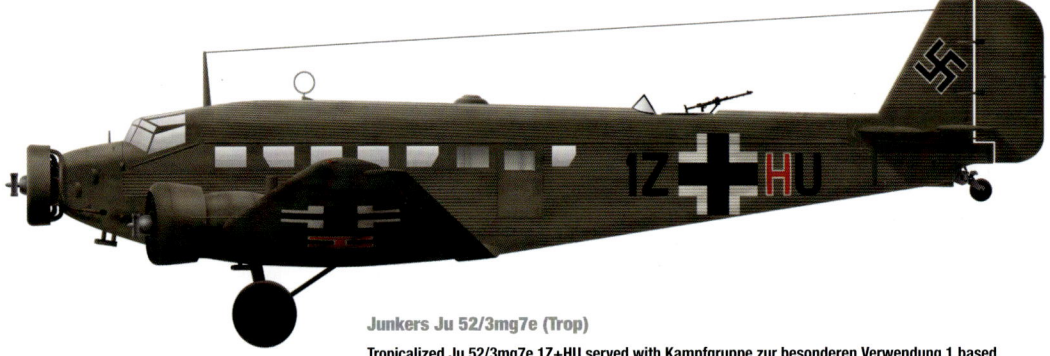

Junkers Ju 52/3mg7e (Trop)
Tropicalized Ju 52/3mg7e 1Z+HU served with Kampfgruppe zur besonderen Verwendung 1 based in the North African theatre from 1942 until early 1943. This aircraft had a cabin air inlet mounted above the fuselage.

established at the Amiot factory in Colombes, France, from where aircraft began to be delivered from June 1942. Additional capacity was generated by PIRT in Budapest, where German-supplied components were used to build another 26 Ju 52/3m aircraft; all but four of these aircraft were delivered to the Hungarian Air Force.

Junkers Ju 52/3 mg7e

Ju 52/3mg7e 1Z+NA served with Stab IV.Transportgeschwader 1 (formerly Kampfgruppe zur besonderen Verwendung 1) on the Courland Front during winter 1944/45. At this stage in the war, the Ju 52/3ms of Stab IV./TG 1 were used for parachuting supplies to Wehrmacht forces.

By the time production came to an end in mid-1944, a total of almost 5000 examples had been built in France and Germany. Post-war production took place in France (as the AAC.1 Toucan) and in Spain, where CASA produced the type for the Spanish Air Force as the CASA 352.

Further developments of the basic design included the Ju 252 and the redesigned Ju 352. The former was a 35-seat passenger transport trimotor developed for Lufthansa and which featured a hydraulically operated ventral loading door. In the event, only 15 examples were built, and it failed to displace the Ju 52/3m. The Ju 352 Herkules was broadly similar to the Ju

Junkers Ju 52/3 mg7e
Weight (Maximum take-off) 11,030kg (24,317lb)
Dimensions Length: 19.90m (62ft), Wingspan: 29.20m (95ft 10in), Height: 4.52m (14ft 10in)
Powerplant Three 619kW (830hp) BMW 132T-2 nine-cylinder radial engines
Speed 286km/h (178mph)
Range 1305km (811 miles)
Ceiling 5900m (19,360ft)
Crew 2/3, plus 18 troops or 12 stretchers
Armament One 7.92mm (0.31in) MG 15 machine gun or 13mm (0.51in) MG 131 machine gun (dorsal)

252 and introduced a mixed wood-and-steel construction with fabric covering to reduce the demand on much-needed aluminium alloys. A total of 33 production Ju 352s were built.

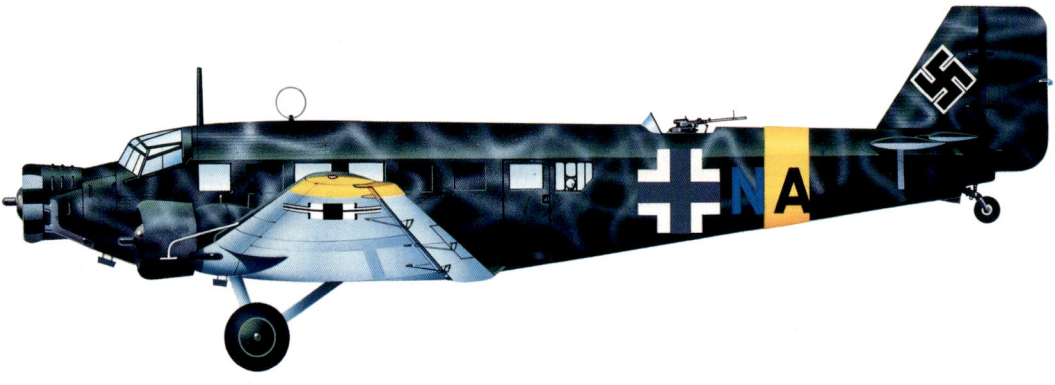

DFS 230

The DFS 230 began life as a military research glider, with a contract being issued for a single prototype that proved successful during flight trials in 1937.

Limited production of an initial DFS 230A series followed and ultimately in excess of 1000 examples were completed, with production being handled by Gothaer Waggonfabrik.

The glider was primarily intended for use as an assault transport and was configured as a braced high-wing monoplane of mixed construction. Accommodation was provided for a crew of two and eight fully equipped troops. The glider could be towed aloft by a variety of Luftwaffe aircraft, taking off with the aid of jettisonable landing gear and returning to land on a central skid mounted below the centre of the fuselage.

Production series
The initial-production DFS 230A-1 was followed by the A-2, a dual-control trainer version, before production switched to the DFS 230B series, including the DFS 230B-1 transport fitted with a braking parachute and the DFS 230B-2 trainer version. The DFS 230C-1 was a further development of the B-series, with three braking rockets in a redesigned nose. The DFS 230 V7 prototype was adapted to carry 15 troops but did not enter production.

Examples of the DFS 230 were involved in the first operation by German gliderborne troops when the Belgian fort at Eben-Emael was captured on 10 May 1940. The DFS 230 also saw use in the invasion of Crete (May 1941) and the rescue of Italian leader Benito Mussolini from his imprisonment in a hotel high in the Apennine Mountains on 12 September 1943. Many DFS 230s were also employed in resupply missions on the Eastern Front.

DFS 230
Here a DFS 230 combat glider is towed by a Dornier Do 17E using a *Starrschlepp* rigid tow.

DFS 230
Weight (Maximum take-off) 2100kg (4630lb)
Dimensions Length: 11.24m (36ft 11in), Wingspan: 21.98m (72ft 1in), Height: 2.74m (9ft)
Powerplant N/A
Speed 290km/h (180mph)
Range N/A
Ceiling N/A
Crew 1, plus 9 equipped troops and 270kg (600lb) cargo
Armament Optional: one 7.92mm (0.31in) MG 15 machine gun (manually mounted aft of cockpit); two 7.92mm (0.31in) MG 34 machine guns (fixed forward firing)

TRANSPORTS AND GLIDERS

Junkers Ju 290

The Ju 290 emerged from the Ju 89 four-engine bomber, three prototypes of which were under construction as of 1936.

The bomber was cancelled the following year and Junkers instead developed a civil version as the Ju 90, which allied the wings and tail assembly of the bomber with a new fuselage. The initial prototype, Ju 90 V1 (D-AALU), completed its maiden flight on 28 August 1937. There followed another three prototypes and 10 pre-production Ju 90B-1 aircraft that were outfitted as 38/40-seat airliners.

The manufacturer was also working on a refined Ju 90S version, with a new wing, sturdier twin-wheel undercarriage, enlarged vertical fins and a ventral loading ramp. It had been planned for the Ju 90S to be powered by four BMW 139 engines, but when these failed to materialize it switched to the BMW 801 and led to a change in designation – the Ju 290.

The initial prototype for this was the reworked Ju 90 V4, while the Ju 90 V7 featured an extended fuselage for additional payload and which also rectified yaw and centre of gravity problems. The Ju 90 V8 was the first prototype to feature defensive armament, with guns in a dorsal turret, tail, under-nose gondola (both forward and rearwards-firing weapons) and waist positions. The final modifications on the path to the productionized Ju 290 were found in the Ju 90 V11 prototype (later renamed Ju 290 V1), which introduced angular fins and redesigned windows and wing. The first flight of this aircraft took place in August 1942.

The first two Ju 290A-0 pre-production aircraft were followed by five examples of the Ju 290A-1, an armed transport, while the Ju 290A-2 was the first of the long-range maritime reconnaissance subvariants, adding an aft dorsal turret, revised navigation equipment and FuG 200 Hohentwiel search radar; three were built. After five Ju 290A-3s had been completed with low-drag Focke-Wulf gun turrets, there

Junkers Ju 290A-5

This aircraft flew with Fernaufklärungsgruppe 5 from Mont-de-Marsan in France. With never more than 20 operational aircraft, the unit struggled to fulfil its commitments in the anti-shipping role.

Junkers Ju 290A-5
Weight (Maximum take-off) 44,969kg (99,140lb)
Dimensions Length: 28.64m (94ft), Wingspan: 42m (137ft 10in), Height: 6.83m (22ft 5in)
Powerplant Four 1300kW (1700hp) BMW 801D 14-cylinder air-cooled radial piston engines
Speed 439km/h (273mph)
Range 6148km (3820 miles)
Ceiling 6000m (19,685ft)
Crew 9
Armament Two 20mm (0.8 in) MG 151/20 cannons (dorsal turrets), one MG 151/20 (tail), two MG 151/20s (waist), one MG 151/20 (gondola), a pair of 13mm (0.51in) MG 131 machine guns (gondola); 3000kg (6600lb) of disposable stores

followed a similar number of Ju 290A-4 aircraft, with another Focke-Wulf gun turret in the forward dorsal position.

TRANSPORTS AND GLIDERS

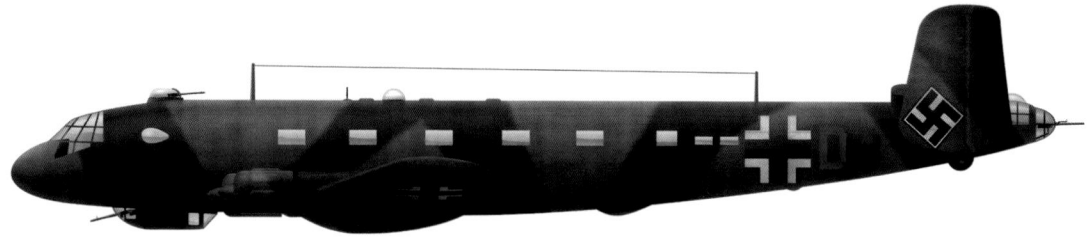

Shortcomings encountered in these initial subvariants were addressed in the subsequent Ju 290A-5, which added protection for the fuel tanks, armour around the flight crew and improved waist gun positions. The crew complement was increased from seven to nine, adding dedicated gunners. The Ju 290A-5 was the most prolific subvariant, the first of 11 entering service in spring 1944.

A key feature of the Ju 290 was the *Trapoklappe*, a hydraulically-operated ramp that raised the cabin to the level position for ground loading, while also providing a ramp for vehicles to drive straight up into the cabin.

After these reconnaissance and maritime reconnaissance versions, the Ju 290A-6 was a one-off 50-seat passenger transport, while the Ju 290A-7 was a reconnaissance/bomber with equipment to launch Henschel Hs 293 or Hs 294 missiles or SD 1400X (Fritz-X) guided bombs. The Ju 290A-8 was developed alongside the A-7, adding two further dorsal gun positions and a twin-gun tail turret. Three Ju 290A-9 aircraft were also built – these were extended-range maritime patrol aircraft with extra internal fuel and a reduced defensive armament.

The final version to be built was the single Ju 290B-1, a prototype long-range, high-altitude heavy bomber that

Junkers Ju 290A-6

Assigned to I./Kampfgeschwader 200, the one-off Ju 290A-6 is seen as it appeared in Barcelona, Spain, in April 1945. Conceived as Hitler's personal transport, the aircraft was flown to Spain in the final weeks of the war, probably carrying a number of high-ranking Nazi officials.

took to the air in 1944. Mention should also be made of the Ju 390, essentially a scaled-up Ju 290 with a wingspan of 55.35m (181ft 7in) and a powerplant of six 1268kW (1700hp) BMW 801D engines. Two prototypes were tested in 1943, but a production order was not forthcoming.

Total production of the Ju 290 amounted to between 60 and 70 aircraft.

TRANSPORTS AND GLIDERS

Arado Ar 232

Design work on the Ar 232 began in early 1940 with the aim of producing a new-generation transport to supplement and eventually succeed the Luftwaffe's Junkers Ju 52/3m.

As of 1 September 1939 when Germany invaded Poland, there were more than 500 examples of the Junkers trimotor still in military service, but the type was already showing its age. The Ar 232, in contrast, was a much more modern proposition, a twin-engine transport with a pod-and-boom fuselage layout and a hydraulically-operated rear loading door.

Unusual undercarriage

To support its weight, the aircraft utilized an unorthodox undercarriage arrangement with no fewer than 11 pairs of small mainwheels. To aid loading and unloading, the tricycle-type landing gear could be raised slightly using a pair of hydraulic rams. This arrangement led to the nickname *Tausendfüssler* – 'millipede'. The Arado design would face competition from the Junkers Ju 252 and Ju 352 (also trimotors) and the six-engine Messerschmitt Me 323A.

The initial two prototypes – the Ar 232 V1 and V2 – took to the air in 1941, and were each powered by a pair of 1193kW (1600hp) BMW 801MA radial engines. However, the demand for engines to support the Focke-Wulf Fw 190 fighter production effort meant that the powerplant had to be switched in subsequent aircraft. The choice fell upon the BMW-Bramo 323R-2, but this offered less power – 895kW (1200hp) – meaning that four engines were now needed.

Third prototype

To accommodate the four-engine powerplant, the third prototype (Ar 232 V3) added an increase in the span of the wing centre section, which was extended by 1.70m (5ft 7in).

Arado Ar 232B

This aircraft, the ninth B-series Ar 232B, J4+UH, was active at Mühldorf, Germany, in summer 1944. The operating unit was Lufttransportstaffel 5.

Arado Ar 232B
Weight (Maximum take-off) 21,150kg (46,628lb)
Dimensions Length: 23.52m (77ft 2in), Wingspan: 33.5m (109ft 11in), Height: 5.69m (18ft 8in)
Powerplant Four 895kW (1200hp) BMW Bramo 323R-2 Fafnir 9-cylinder radial piston engines
Speed 308km/h (191mph)
Range 1062km (660 miles)
Ceiling 6900m (22,600ft)
Crew 4
Armament One 13mm (0.51in) MG 131 machine gun (nose), one 20mm (0.8in) MG 151/20 autocannon (dorsal turret), one 13mm (0.51 in) MG 131 machine gun (rear position)

TRANSPORTS AND GLIDERS

The Ar 232 was nicknamed *Tausendfüssler* – German for 'millipede' – on account of its unconventional undercarriage, which featured 11 pairs of small mainwheels. Other notable features were the box-like fuselage, rear loading ramp and high-mounted twin tail for easy access to the hold.

Only a handful of pre-production Ar 232A-0 machines were manufactured and most served with a single squadron within the *Ergänzungsgruppe* (replacement transport group) before being passed on to Transportfliegerstaffel 5 in late 1944.

The third prototype served as the first of the Ar 232B-0 pre-production series, of which 20 were eventually completed for the Luftwaffe. These initially saw service with units on the Eastern Front, but later in the war began to be issued to the special missions Kampfgeschwader 200, where Ar 232s were serving as part of 3./KG 200 in March 1945.

Experimental use

Other special tasks assigned to the Ar 232 included evaluating an experimental boundary-layer control system, while another example was flown with four 522kW (700hp) Gnome-Rhône 14M radial engines. One more example was completed with an experimental ski landing gear intended for use in Norway.

At the end of the war in Europe a single aircraft from 3./KG 200 was flown from its base at Flensburg to Farnborough in the United Kingdom, where it was tested by the Royal Aircraft Establishment, with favourable results.

Although major airframe sections were finished, no examples of the follow-on Ar 432 were ever completed. This would have been a further development of the Ar 232 with wood and steel replacing the previous light alloys, which were becoming increasingly hard to obtain as the war in Europe drew to a close.

TRANSPORTS AND GLIDERS

Messerschmitt Me 323 *Gigant*

The Me 323 heavy transport was derived from a transport glider design once intended to spearhead an airborne invasion of the United Kingdom. It was capable of carrying tanks, artillery and troops.

This aircraft was the Me 321, work on which continued after the invasion of the UK was abandoned, with a view to deploying it on the Eastern Front instead. Contracts were issued to both Junkers (the all-wing Ju 322) and Messerschmitt (the more conventional Me 321), but in the event the former was cancelled.

The prototype Me 321 could carry loads of up to 20,000kg (44,092lb) or up to 200 troops in a cargo hold that measured 11m (36ft 1in) long, 3.30m (10ft 10in) wide and 3.15m (10ft 4in) high. The glider was fitted with a jettisonable take-off dolly and rocket-assisted take-off gear, returning to land on sprung skids.

A first flight occurred on 25 February 1941, after being carried aloft behind a Ju 90. Although the aircraft handled satisfactorily, the Ju 90 was inadequate as a tug and there were a number of early accidents

Messerschmitt Me 323E-2 Gigant
A Me 323E-2 operated by I./Kampfgruppe zur besonderen Verwendung 323, operating in Italy in spring 1943. The unit was later designated Transportgeschwader 5 and served on the Eastern Front.

that occurred in the take-off phase. Despite this, a total of 100 Me 323A-1 production gliders was completed, followed by a similar number of Me 321B-1 gliders with a wider flight deck for pilot and co-pilot. Production of these was completed by early 1942, by which time the Heinkel He 111Z was available as a tug.

Powered version
Continued problems on take-off led to the decision to develop a powered version, the Me 232, and the two prototype Me 321s were duly converted to serve as development aircraft for the Me 323C and Me 323D,

Messerschmitt Me 323D-1 Gigant
Weight (Maximum take-off) 43,000kg (94,799lb)
Dimensions Length: 28.2m (92ft 6in), Wingspan: 55.2m (181ft 1in), Height: 10.15m (33ft 4in)
Powerplant Six 868kW (1164hp) Gnome-Rhône 14N-48 14-cylinder radial piston engines
Speed 285km/h (177mph)
Range 1000km (620 miles)
Ceiling 4000m (13,000ft)
Crew 5, plus 120 troops or 9750kg (21,495lb) load
Armament Two 7.92mm (0.31in) MG 15, MG 81 or 13mm (0.51in) MG 131 machine guns in cockpit, two 7.92mm (0.31in) MG 15s in waist (optional)

which featured four or six Gnome-Rhône 14N radial engines respectively. Since the four-engine Me 323C still required a tug to get aloft, work on this variant was terminated.

Instead, the Me 323D began to be produced in series from August 1942

TRANSPORTS AND GLIDERS

and made its operational debut in support of Axis troops in North Africa in November that year. It could carry a load of 9750kg (21,495lb), or 120 fully-equipped troops, or 60 stretcher patients plus attendants, over a distance of more than 1000km (621 miles).

Operating procedure saw as many as 100 Me 323 and Ju 52/3m transports launched simultaneously with fighter escort, and while this strategy was initially successful, increasing Allied fighter opposition soon made such tactics obsolete. On one occasion in mid-April 1943, a formation of no fewer than 16 Me 323s was attacked by RAF fighters, and all but two of the German transports were destroyed.

Me 323E

Additional armament and armour produced the Me 323E production series, with two additional turrets each carrying a pair of 20mm (0.8in) MG 151/20 cannons, and two additional gunners to operate them. But the *Gigant* was eventually withdrawn from the Mediterranean theatre to see out the remainder of the war on the Eastern Front.

The final Me 323F production series was re-engined with six 1007kW (1350hp) Junkers Jumo 21R powerplants.

A total of 198 examples had been delivered by the time production ended in April 1944 and it seems the type was removed from frontline service soon after this date.

The *Gigant* was versatile and could carry a range of cargo. Different combat zones called for different types of supplies. For example, on the Eastern Front, horses were needed to pull gun carriages and other heavy equipment on muddy, unpaved roads (see top left); while a whole company of paratroopers could be carried in the air assault role (lower left). Single light armoured vehicles, such as an SdKfz 251 halftrack, could also be transported to add mobile support to a deployment (see above).

87

Gotha Go 242 and Go 244

The Go 242 assault glider was designed by Albert Kalkert with the approval of the *Reichsluftfahrtministerium* (German Air Ministry) and was intended as a successor to the DFS 230 but offering almost three times the load-carrying capacity.

Based on a fuselage of steel tubular construction with fabric covering, the Go 242 was fitted with jettisonable wheeled landing gear and a pair of retractable skids. The wooden wings also had fabric covering. The glider offered accommodation for 21 fully equipped troops or a military cargo, such as a Kübelwagen utility vehicle, loaded/unloaded via a hinged rear fuselage.

Two prototypes were flown in 1941 and were followed by the initial production Go 242A version, first used in combat in the Mediterranean and Aegean in 1942. The gliders were usually carried aloft by Heinkel He 111s, with rocket-assisted take-off gear also available. The follow-on Go 242B series introduced jettisonable nosewheel undercarriage and included the Go 242B-5 dual-control trainer, while the planned Go 242C was intended for attacks on marine targets and would have featured a boat-like hull and underwing floats.

As well as production of 1528 Go 242 gliders, work began on providing a powerplant, in the form of a pair of 522kW (700hp) Gnome-Rhône 14M radial engines. The resulting Go 244 incorporated tricycle landing gear and an engine nacelle in each of the extended twin booms.

A total of 133 conversions were made from different Go 242B variants, and deliveries began in March 1942, initially to units based in Greece and Crete. However, the Go 244 proved vulnerable to fighter interception and it had been withdrawn by November the same year.

Gotha Go 244B-1
Weight (gross) 7800kg (17,196lb)
Dimensions Length: 15.8m (51ft 10in), Wingspan: 24.5m (80ft 5in), Height: 4.7m (15ft 5in)
Powerplant Two 522kW (700hp) Gnome-Rhône 14M radial engines
Speed 290km/h (180 mph)
Range 600km (370 miles)
Ceiling 7500m (24,600ft)
Crew 2, plus up to 21 troops or freight

Siebel Si 204

The Fh 104 and Si 204 were designed and developed by the Siebel company in Germany but were destined to find greater fame after the war when they were manufactured in France as the SNCAC NC.701 and NC.702 Martinet.

The aircraft originated as the Fh 104, a five-seat, all-metal, twin-engine light transport, before being further developed from 1938 as the 10-seat Si 204, which was powered by a pair of Argus As 411 inverted-Vee engines driving two-blade, variable-pitch propellers.

Large-scale production

After 15 prototype aircraft produced at Halle, large-scale manufacture commenced with the pre-production Si 204A-0 and initial-production Si 204A-1 passenger transports produced by SNCAC in France on behalf of Germany. The Si 204D series was a trainer equipped for blind flying and developed by BMM in Czechoslovakia; a first Si 204D-0 pre-series aircraft was delivered in January 1943 and was followed by another 44 Si 204D-1 production aircraft from the Aero and BMM factories. In an effort to relieve pressure on the aluminium supplies, the Si 204D-3 substituted wooden wings and tailplanes for the original metal parts.

It has been suggested that an example of the Si 204 was the last

Siebel Si 204E
Weight (Maximum take-off) 5600kg (12,346lb)
Dimensions Length: 11.95m (39ft 2in), Wingspan: 21.33m (70ft), Height: 4.25m (13ft 11in)
Powerplant Two 440kW (590hp) Argus As 411-A1 V-12 inverted-V air-cooled piston engines
Speed 364km/h (226mph)
Range 1800km (1100 miles)
Ceiling 7500m (24,600ft)
Crew 1 or 2, plus 8 passengers
Armament One 7.92mm (0.31in) machine gun in turret aft of the cockpit

TRANSPORTS AND GLIDERS

German aircraft shot down in the Western theatre during World War II. On the evening of 8 May 1945, an example was downed by a US Army Air Force (USAAF) P-38 Lightning, southeast of Rodach in Bavaria.

Total wartime production was 1216 aircraft, including the prototypes.

In addition to French post-war production, others continued to be manufactured by Aero in Czechoslovakia, where the type was produced as the military C.3 trainer and D.44 transport (until 1949), as well as the civilian C.103 passenger variant.

Siebel Si 204D-0
This Si 204D-0 wears the codes of Kampfgeschwader 200 – the Luftwaffe's special duties wing. One of the unit's Siebels was used by 2./KG 200 in support of Albert Speer's peace negotiations in April 1945.

Siebel Si 204E
A Si 204E of 2./Nachtschlachtgruppe 4, based at Malacky, Slovakia, in 1944. These aircraft were used for psychological warfare tasks, including leaflet dropping, as well as in the more usual role of *Staffel* or *Gruppe* liaison aircraft.

Siebel Si 204D-1
Wearing the codes of 2./Seeaufklärungsgruppe 126 and equipped with Hohentwiel maritime search radar, this Si 204D-1 escaped the advancing Allied armies on 19 April 1945, flying to Bredåkra, Sweden.

SEAPLANES AND MARITIME AIRCRAFT

The emergence of the maritime strike role brought about the demand for the adaptation of often obsolescent fighter, bomber and transport aircraft to meet operational requirements. Seaplanes and flying boats, meanwhile, provided another means of prosecuting a range of maritime tasks, from mine warfare and anti-shipping strikes to air-sea rescue, as well as clandestine roles, such as delivering agents to hostile coastlines.

This chapter includes the following:

- Heinkel He 59
- Heinkel He 60
- Dornier Do 18
- Dornier Do 24
- Blohm und Voss Ha 139
- Focke-Wulf Fw 200
- Arado Ar 95
- Arado Ar 196
- Dornier Do 26
- Fieseler Fi 167
- Blohm und Voss BV 138
- Blohm und Voss BV 222
- Heinkel He 114
- Heinkel He 115
- Blohm und Voss BV 238

The ground crew of a Heinkel He 115 seaplane load an F5b 45cm (17in) torpedo into the bomb bay before a combat sortie.

SEAPLANES AND MARITIME AIRCRAFT

Heinkel He 59

The He 59 was designed as a reconnaissance-bomber and initially schemed as either a floatplane or a landplane with wheeled undercarriage.

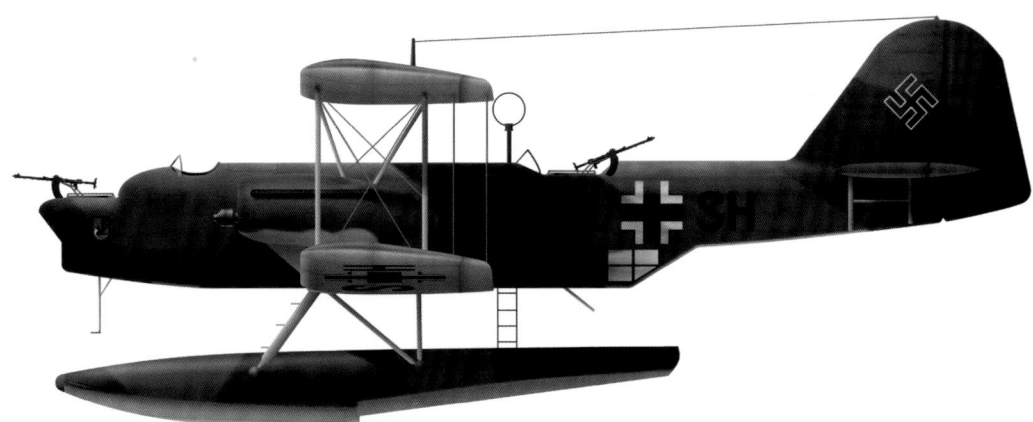

The He 59b second prototype was completed with faired wheeled landing gear and first flew in September 1931. It was followed into the air by the first prototype, the He 59a, which was fitted with twin single-step floats. A small batch of unarmed He 59A aircraft were produced for evaluation, these being to the same standard as the He 59a. The subsequent production aircraft were all built as floatplanes, most of them being produced by Arado, and were powered by a pair of 492kW (660hp) BMW VI 6.0ZU engines.

The type entered service in 1933 and saw operational trials in Spain in 1936. By the outbreak of World War II, the Luftwaffe was operating the type with coastal reconnaissance units for roles including multi-role trainer, air-sea rescue and as a minelayer.

He 59B-1

The 16 initial-production He 59B-1 aircraft featured minor equipment changes and were armed with a 7.92mm (0.31in) MG 15 machine gun in the nose, while the He 59B-2 had an all-metal nose with glazed panels for the bomb-aimer and an extra MG 15 in a glazed ventral position.

When deployed with the Condor Legion in Spain, the He 59B-2 carried a 20mm (0.8in) MG FF cannon in the nose for anti-shipping patrols. The He 59B-3 was a reconnaissance version with nose gun deleted and with auxiliary fuel tanks in the fuselage.

He 59C-1

The He 59C-1 was a stripped-down long-range reconnaissance model, while the unarmed He 59C-2 carried six dinghies for air-sea rescue operations. The He 59D was similar to the He 59C-2, while the He 59D-1 was a crew trainer. Similar to the He 59D-1, the He 59E-1 was a trainer outfitted for torpedo launch, while three He 59E-2 aircraft were completed with cameras for reconnaissance. Finally, a number of He 59D-1 aircraft were also converted for use as advanced navigation trainers, becoming He 95N aircraft.

Heinkel He 59B-1

A He 59 assigned to I./Kustenfliegergruppe 906 based at Levanger, Norway, around 1940.

Heinkel He 59B-1

Weight (Maximum take-off) 9119kg (20,104lb)
Dimensions Length 17.4m (57ft 1in), Wingspan: 23.7m (77ft 9in), Height: 7.1m (23ft 4in)
Powerplant Two 492kW (660hp) BMW VI 6.0ZU V-12 piston engines
Speed 221km/h (137mph)
Range 942km (585 miles)
Ceiling 3500m (11,500ft)
Crew 4
Armament Two 7.92mm (0.31in) MG 15 machine guns; two 500kg (1100lb) or four 250kg (551lb) bombs

Heinkel He 60

The He 60 was devised as a catapult-capable reconnaissance and spotting floatplane for operations from larger Kriegsmarine warships.

The initial He 60a prototype was flown in 1933 powered by a 492kW (660hp) BMW VI engine. It was replaced by the second prototype, the He 60b, with the same engine uprated to 559kW (750hp). The revised powerplant did not offer any significant benefit and was not adopted for subsequent aircraft, including the third prototype, the He 60c, which was equipped for catapult launching. This aircraft undertook trials to confirm its suitability for shipborne service.

Active service
In 1933 the first examples of the He 60A entered service with the Kriegsmarine's training schools, this version being unarmed. A total of 14 of these He 60A pre-production machines were completed. Operational He 60B versions then began to be used aboard German battleships and cruisers. A single He 60B-3 was completed for evaluation with the 671kW (900hp) Daimler-Benz B 600 engine, while an improved version of the He 60B was completed as the He 60C, introduced in 1934. The He 60D was an unarmed trainer.

Second-line duties
Quite early in World War II, the He 60 was demoted to second-line duties but it remained in service longer among maritime reconnaissance units serving in Greece and Crete. In 1941 the type returned to frontline service to operate along the coastal flank of the German armies invading the Soviet Union from June, but was once again phased out of frontline service between June and October 1943.

The He 60E designation applied to six He 60D-standard aircraft that were supplied to Spain; four of these survived in service as late as 1948.

Heinkel He 60D
This He 60D was on strength with 1./Seeaufklärungsgruppe 126, based at Kalamata, Greece, around 1941.

Heinkel He 60D
Weight (Maximum take-off) 3407kg (7511lb)
Dimensions Length: 11.5m (37ft 9in), Wingspan: 13.5m (44ft 3in), Height: 5.3m (17ft 5in)
Powerplant One 492kW (660hp) BMW VI 6.0 V-12 piston engine
Speed 240km/h (150mph)
Range 826km (513 miles)
Ceiling 5000m (16,000ft)
Crew 2
Armament Capability added for a fixed 7.92mm (0.31in) MG 17 machine gun in rear cockpit

SEAPLANES AND MARITIME AIRCRAFT

Dornier Do 18

The Dornier Do 18 was developed as a successor to the well-received Dornier *Wal* family of interwar flying boats and was originally designed in 1934 to serve Lufthansa as a transatlantic mail plane.

More aerodynamically efficient than its predecessors, the Do 18 employed the same basic metal hull and stabilising sponsons. The initial Do 18a prototype, powered by two 493kW (540hp) Junkers Jumo 5 diesel engines, took to the air for the first time on 15 March 1935. It was followed by four Do 18E aircraft, each powered by a pair of 447kW (600hp) Jumo 205C engines. The sixth aircraft, also for Lufthansa, was the sole Do 18F, first flown in June 1937 and used to establish a seaplane distance record, flying 8391 kilometres (5214 miles) between England and Brazil the following year. The same aircraft was later modified as the Do 18L, fitted with a pair of 656kW (880hp) BMW 132N engines.

Active service

The Do 18D-1 entered service with Luftwaffe coastal reconnaissance units in September 1938, powered by Jumo 205C engines and armed with single 7.92mm (0.31in) machine guns in open bow and dorsal positions.

Dornier Do 18D-1
This Do 18D-1 served with 2./Küstenfliegergruppe 906 in Pomerania, in the winter of 1939–40.

An aircraft of this type was the first German military airplane brought down by British forces in World War II, an example from 2./Küstenfliegergruppe 106 being downed by Blackburn Skuas of the Fleet Air Arm's 803 Squadron on 26 September 1939.

The improved Do 18G-1 featured 656kW (880hp) Jumo 205D engines and was armed with a 20mm (0.8in) MG 151/20 cannon in a power-operated dorsal turret and a 13mm (0.51in) machine gun in the bow.

Air-sea rescue

A total of just over 100 Do 18s were completed by 1940 and after replacement by the BV 138, the type continued in use on air-sea rescue duties from 1942, including examples of the unarmed Do 18N-1, which were converted for the role from the Do 18G-1.

Dornier Do 18D-1
Weight (Maximum take-off) 8500kg (18,739lb)
Dimensions Length: 19.23m (63ft 1in) Wingspan: 23.7m (77ft 9in), Height: 5.32m (17ft 5in)
Powerplant Two 447kW (600hp) Junkers Jumo 205C-4 six-cylinder diesel engines
Speed 250km/h (160mph)
Range 3500km (2200 miles)
Ceiling 4350m (14,270ft)
Crew 4
Armament Two 7.92mm (0.31in) MG 15 machine guns; two 50kg (110lb) or two 100kg (220lb) bombs

Dornier Do 24

The Dornier Do 24 was developed to meet a Dutch requirement of 1935 for a flying boat to replace the Dornier *Wal* in use in the Netherlands East Indies.

The Do 24 was equipped with a strut-mounted wing carrying three engines and it combined all-metal construction with a shallow, broad-beamed hull and stabilizing sponsons. The first two prototypes were tailored to meet a potential German military requirement and were powered by 447kW (600hp) Junkers Jumo 205C diesel engines.

However, they were preceded into the air by the third prototype, which made a maiden flight on 3 July 1937, with a powerplant of two 652kW (875hp) Wright R-1820-F52 Cyclone engines, to meet the Dutch requirement for commonality with its Martin 139 bombers.

The fourth prototype was also completed to the Dutch standard. After successful completion of the test programme, the aircraft entered production for the Netherlands at Dornier's Altenrhein plant, under the designation Do 24K-1.

A further 48 aircraft were to be completed under licence in the Netherlands by Aviolanda, while the

Dornier Do 24K-2
This Dutch-built Do 24K-2 was completed for the Luftwaffe for air-sea rescue duties.

wings would be produced by De Schelde. In the event, the production run of these Do 24K-2 aircraft was cut short by the outbreak of the war, and only 25 were delivered before German forces occupied the country in May 1940. The Do 24K-2 differed in its powerplant of three 746kW (1000hp) Wright R-1820-G102 engines.

Evaluation
After the German invasion, three examples of the Do 24K-2 were transferred to Germany for evaluation, together with a number of unfinished airframes from the Dutch production line. After successful testing in the air-sea rescue role, production was reinstated at the Aviolanda works, now under the control of the German Weser Flugzeugbau. Production amounted to 170 aircraft for Luftwaffe use,

Dornier Do 24K-2
Weight (Maximum take-off) 18,400kg (40,565lb)
Dimensions Length: 22.05m (72ft 4in), Wingspan: 27m (88ft 7in), Height: 5.75m (18ft 10in)
Powerplant Three 746kW (1000hp) Wright R-1820-G102 engines
Speed 330km/h (210mph)
Range 2900km (1800 miles)
Ceiling 7500m (24,600ft)
Crew 4 or 6
Armament N/A

SEAPLANES AND MARITIME AIRCRAFT

beginning with 11 Dutch-built Do 24N-1 aircraft that were completed to the same standard as the Do 24K-2, retaining the R-1820-G102 engines. The first example was delivered to the Luftwaffe in August 1941 and these aircraft served in the air-sea rescue role.

Further production in the Netherlands yielded the Do 24T series, which were now powered by three 746kW (1000hp) BMW-Bramo 323R-2 Fafnir engines. The primary operator of these 159 Do 24T-1, T-2 and T-3 aircraft, which featured minor equipment changes, were 1., 2., and 3./Seenotgruppe based at Biscarrosse, near Bordeaux, and Berre, near Marseilles. Armament of the T-series comprised a 20mm (0.8in) MG 151/20 cannon in a power-operated dorsal turret and single 7.92mm (0.31in) MG 15 machine guns in each of the bow and tail positions.

French factory

The flying boat was also built in France by the SNCA du Nord factory at Sartrouville, between 1942 and August 1944. Another 40 aircraft were delivered to the French navy following the end of the war.

A total of 12 Do 24T-3 aircraft were delivered to Spain under the local designation HR.5, deliveries beginning in June 1944. These were to enjoy a remarkably long career in the air-sea rescue role, remaining in service at Pollensa, Majorca, into the 1970s. One other wartime variant was the single Do 318 prototype that was modified by Weser in 1944 with an Arado-designed boundary-layer control system. This aircraft completed a successful evaluation programme on Lake Constance where it was finally scuttled in 1945.

The third prototype, Do 24 V3, was registered as D-ADLP and powered by Wright Cyclones. First flown in July 1937, it was officially handed over to the Dutch Navy for acceptance trials and later shipped to Java, where it entered service as X-1 – the first of the Dutch Do 24Ks.

Dornier Do 24T-2

This Do 24T-2 of the 7.Seenotstaffel/SBK XI, flew in the Aegean area in 1942.

Dornier Do 24T-2

Weight (Maximum take-off) 18,400kg (40,565lb)
Dimensions Length: 22.05m (72ft 4in), Wingspan: 27m (88ft 7in), Height: 5.75m (18ft 10in)
Powerplant Three 746kW (1000hp) Bramo 323R-2 Fafnir nine-cylinder radial piston engines
Speed 330km/h (210mph)
Range 2900km (1800 miles)
Ceiling 7500m (24,600ft)
Crew 4 or 6
Armament One 20mm (0.8in) MG 151/20 cannon (dorsal turret) and two 7.92mm (0.31in) MG 15 machine guns (nose and tail)

Blohm und Voss Ha 139

Developed to serve Lufthansa's newly established transatlantic postal service, the Ha 139 was a four-engine long-range floatplane first flown in prototype form in autumn 1936.

This aircraft had been tailored to operate from rough water and be suitable for catapult launch with a payload of 500kg (1102lb).

The first two examples had been delivered to Lufthansa by March 1937 and began operating between the Azores and New York. The first two aircraft were briefly removed from service in November 1937 to be retrofitted with enlarged vertical tail surfaces to improve directional stability, and underwing radiators on all four Junkers Jumo 205 engines to address cooling problems. A third aircraft was completed to a slightly modified design, as the Ha 139B, which entered service in mid-1938.

Luftwaffe service

With the outbreak of the war, the Ha 139s and their crews were absorbed by the Luftwaffe. The third machine – the former Ha 139B – was modified for reconnaissance duties with a lengthened glazed nose to accommodate an observer; to compensate for this, the vertical tail surfaces were enlarged. The former Ha 139B was re-designated as the Ha 139V3/U1 and received armament befitting its new military role: four 7.92mm (0.31in) MG 17 machine guns in each of the nose, dorsal and twin beam positions.

Minesweeper

The Ha 139V3/U1 subsequently saw service as a minesweeper with a degaussing loop energized by field-generating equipment accommodated in the fuselage; with this change, the aircraft now became the Ha 139B/MS.

All three aircraft saw operational service during the Norwegian campaign in 1940, the first two serving in the troop transport role.

Blohm und Voss Ha 139B/MS

Configured as a minesweeper, this Ha 139B/MS was operational in 1940.

Blohm und Voss Ha 139B/MS

Weight (Maximum take-off) 19,000kg (41,888lb)
Dimensions Length: 20.07m (65ft 10in), Wingspan: 29.5m (96ft 9in), Height: 4.8m (15ft 9in)
Powerplant Four 447kW (599hp) Junkers Jumo 205C six-cylinder diesel engines
Speed 288km/h (179mph)
Range 4600km (2858 miles)
Ceiling 7620m (25,000ft)
Crew 4 or 5
Armament Four 7.92mm (0.31in) MG 15 machine guns (nose, dorsal and twin beam positions)

SEAPLANES AND MARITIME AIRCRAFT

Focke-Wulf Fw 200 *Kondor*

The brainchild of aeronautical engineer Kurt Tank, the Fw 200 was schemed as a transport for Deutsche Lufthansa and the design was submitted to the airline in July 1936.

In the meantime, Focke-Wulf had begun work on the first of three prototypes, the Fw 200 V1, which took to the air on 27 July 1937. An all-metal low-wing monoplane, in its initial form it was powered by four 652kW (875hp) Pratt & Whitney Hornet radial engines and was intended to accommodate 26 passengers. Another two prototypes were completed with four 537kW (720hp) BMW 132G-1 radials each, and one of these became a personal transport for Adolf Hitler. Meanwhile, the second prototype and four examples of the initial-production Fw 200A were delivered to Deutsche Lufthansa and another two were exported for commercial service in Brazil.

Fw 200 V10 prototype

Further examples had been delivered to Lufthansa before the outbreak of the war. On the military side, the Fw 200 V10 prototype was built, offering increased fuel capacity and a defensive armament of a 7.92mm (0.31in) MG 15 machine gun in a dorsal turret and another two similar weapons firing fore and aft from a ventral gondola. The Fw 200 V10 served as the pattern aircraft for the Luftwaffe's pre-series Fw 200C-0, 10 of which were ordered in September 1939. Four of these served in an unarmed configuration with Kampfgeschwader zur besonderen Verwendung (KGzbV) 105, while the other six were armed with an MG 15 in each of the forward and aft dorsal turrets and a third weapon firing through a ventral hatch.

Norwegian campaign

The C-series first saw military service with KGzbV 105 during the Norwegian campaign. However, the *Kondor* really made its mark in the long-maritime reconnaissance role, proving to be a serious threat to Allied shipping as soon as it was introduced by the Fernaufklärungsstaffel (later 1./Kampfgeschwader 40) in April 1940. The Fw 200 continued in this role until autumn 1944, after which the *Kondor* was used primarily for transport duties for the remainder of the war, its operating unit now including Transportstaffeln 5 and 200 and the Führerkürierstaffel.

In total, around 280 *Kondors* were built, and the military C-series included the initial-production Fw 200C-1

Focke-Wulf Fw 200C-3
An Fw 200C-3 flown by 1./Kampfgeschwader 40 based at Bordeaux-Mérignac, France, in 1940. This *Condor* was posted missing during a mission over the Atlantic on 24 July 1941.

Focke-Wulf Fw 200C-3
Weight (Maximum take-off) 22,714kg (50,076lb)
Dimensions Length: 23.45m (76ft 11in), Wingspan: 32.85m (107ft 9in), Height: 6.3m (20ft 8in)
Powerplant Four 708kW (950hp) Bramo 323R-2 Fafnir nine-cylinder radial piston engines
Speed 380km/h (240mph)
Range 3560km (2210 miles)
Ceiling 6000m (20,000ft)
Crew 5
Armament Four 7.92mm (0.31in) MG 15 machine guns, one 20mm (0.8in) MG 151 cannon; 1000kg (2200lb) bombs internally or up to 5400kg (11,900lb) externally

reconnaissance aircraft with a 20mm (0.8in) MG FF cannon in the nose, one MG 15 in a ventral gondola, a similar weapon in a forward dorsal position and a third in a rear dorsal position. It could also carry four 250kg (551lb) weapons on underwing racks. The Fw 200C-2 was similar, but with the rear of the outboard engine nacelles cut

SEAPLANES AND MARITIME AIRCRAFT

away and provided with streamlined bomb racks.

Fw 200C series

Appearing in 1941, the Fw 200C-3 was structurally strengthened and powered by Bramo 323R-2 radial engines; the Fw 200C-3/U1 sub-variant had a 15mm (0.59in) MG 151 cannon in a revised forward turret and replaced the ventral MG FF with a 20mm (0.8in) MG 151/20. The Fw 200C-3/U2 then replaced the ventral MG 151/20 with an MG 131 and included a Lofte 7D bombsight, while the Fw 200C-3/U3 carried an MG 131 in each of the front and rear dorsal positions; the final Fw 200C-3/U4 sub-variant carried an extra gunner and two additional beam-mounted MG 131s.

The next production version was the Fw 200C-4 that appeared in 1942, with FuG Rostock search radar later replaced by FuG 200 Hohentwiel and armed with an MG 151 in the forward dorsal turret, a ventral MG 151/20 (or MG 131 and Lofte bombsight) and MG 131 and MG 15s at other stations. Single examples were completed as Fw 200C-4/U1 and Fw 200C-4/U2 transports. The missile-carrier version was the Fw 200C-6, produced through

Focke-Wulf Fw 200C-4

Another Kampfgeschwader 40 aircraft, this Fw 200C-4 was on strength with 7./KG 40, operating out of Norway in May 1945.

modification of Fw 200C-3/U1 and Fw 200C-3/U2 aircraft, with provision for two underwing Henschel Hs 293A rocket-propelled guided bombs and missile control equipment; this version entered service with III./KG 40 in November 1943.

Finally, the Fw 200C-8 was the definitive missile carrier, and was equipped with Hohentwiel radar.

Focke-Wulf Fw 200C-4

Weight (Maximum take-off) 22,700kg (50,045lb)
Dimensions Length: 23.85mm (78ft 3in), Wingspan: 32.84m (107ft 9in), Height: 6.3m (20ft 8in)
Powerplant Four 708kW (950hp) Bramo 323R-2 Fafnir nine-cylinder radial piston engines
Speed 360km/h (224mph)
Range 3560km (2212 miles)
Ceiling 6000m (19,685ft)
Crew 7
Armament Four 7.92mm (0.31in) MG 15 machine guns, one 13mm (0.51in) MG 131 machine gun, one 20mm (0.8in) MG 151 cannon; 1000kg (2200lb) bombs internally or up to 5400kg (11,900lb) externally

This Focke-Wulf Fw 200C-3 is equipped with a FuG 200 Hohentwiel radar antenna in the nose. It could detect surface ships up to a range of 70km (43 miles).

SEAPLANES AND MARITIME AIRCRAFT

Focke-Wulf Fw 200C-1 Kondor
Ths aircraft flew anti-convoy missions with 1./KG 40 IV Fliegerkorps, Luftflotte 3, from Bordeaux-Mérignac, France, in 1940.

Crew
The Fw 200C-1 had a crew of five: pilot, co-pilot, flight engineer/gunner, navigator/bombadier (who also doubled as radio operator/gunner), and rear dorsal gunner.

Powerplant
The Fw 200C was powered by the same 620 kW (830hp) BMW 132H air-cooled, nine-cylinder piston engines as its airline progenitor, the Fw 200B-2.

Defensive Armament
The Fw 200C-1 had a gondola that featured a 20mm (0.8in) MG FF cannon on a flexible mounting in the nose and a 7.92mm (0.31in) MG 15 in the tail. Another MG 15 was included in a fixed cupola above the turret, with a further MG 15 in a rear dorsal turret.

SEAPLANES AND MARITIME AIRCRAFT

Focke-Wulf Fw 200C-1
Weight (Maximum take-off) 22,700kg (50,045lb)
Dimensions Length: 23.46m (76ft 11in), Wingspan: 32.82m (107ft 8in), Height: 6.3m (20ft 8in)
Powerplant Four 620kW (830hp) BMW 132H radial piston engines
Speed 360km/h (224mph)
Range 4440km (2795 miles)
Ceiling 6000m (19,685ft)
Crew 5
Armament Three 7.92mm (0.31in) MG 15 machine guns, one 20mm (0.8in) MG FF cannon; four 250kg (551lb) bombs or two 1000kg (2205lb) mines

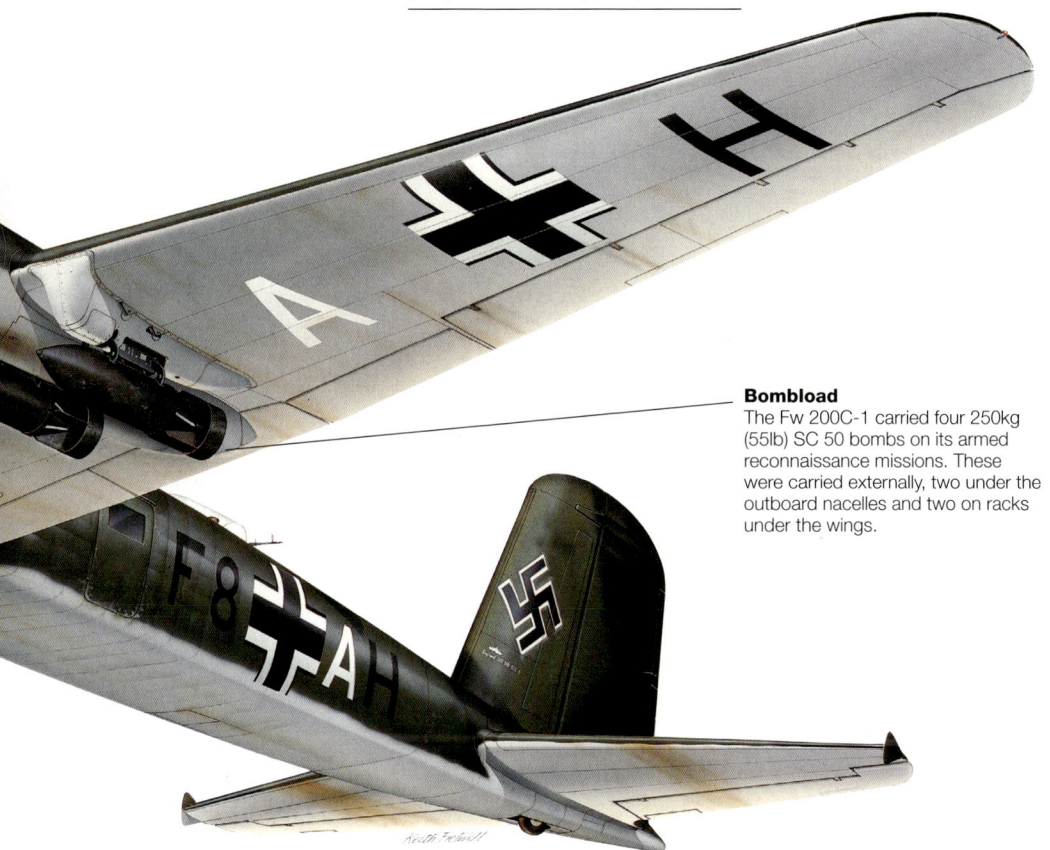

Bombload
The Fw 200C-1 carried four 250kg (55lb) SC 50 bombs on its armed reconnaissance missions. These were carried externally, two under the outboard nacelles and two on racks under the wings.

SEAPLANES AND MARITIME AIRCRAFT

Arado Ar 95

Designed in 1935 by Walter Blume, the Arado Ar 95 was a two-seat, twin-float seaplane of all-metal construction, with parallel-chord wings attached to centre sections of unequal chord and thickness.

As a result of this latter feature, the crew had easy access to the cockpits from the lower wing root, and improved upward visibility thanks to the thinner and narrower upper surface. The side-by-side single-step floats were strut-braced to the fuselage and the lower-wing centre-section. A sliding canopy enclosed the twin cockpits, the rear end of which was left open and featured a 7.92mm (0.31in) MG 17 machine gun; a similar forward-firing weapon was installed in the upper fuselage.

Coastal patrol aircraft

Intended for coastal patrol, reconnaissance and light attack, the first prototype was flown in 1937, powered by a 656kW (880hp) BMW 132De nine-cylinder engine. The second was fitted with a 514kW (690hp) Junkers Jumo 210 12-cylinder engine. These two aircraft took part in a competitive fly-off against the Focke-Wulf Fw 62. Although the BMW-powered version of the Arado design was considered suitable for service, only six prototype and pre-production aircraft were initially completed and used for service trials with the Condor Legion in the Spanish Civil War.

In 1938 a derivative of the floatplane was ordered for Turkey as the Ar 95W, while the Ar 95L with fixed, wheeled landing gear was acquired by Chile. While the Chilean aircraft had been delivered by the outbreak of World War II, those from the Turkish order were diverted to the Luftwaffe as the Ar 95A, serving as trainers within the *Seeaufklärungsgruppen* (coastal reconnaissance groups).

Arado Ar 95A-1

This Ar 95A-1 was part of 13./Seeaufklärungsgruppe 125 that flew missions along the Baltic coast from 1941.

Arado Ar 95A-1

Weight (Maximum take-off) 3560kg (7848lb)
Dimensions Length: 11.10m (36ft 5in), Wingspan: 12.50m (41ft), Height: 3.60m (11ft 10in)
Powerplant One 656kW (880hp) BMW 132De nine-cylinder radial engine
Speed 310km/h (190mph)
Range 1100km (680 miles)
Ceiling 7300m (24,000ft)
Crew 2
Armament One 7.92mm (0.31in) MG 17 machine gun, one 7.92mm (0.31in) MG 15 machine gun, one 800kg (1764lb) torpedo or one 500kg (1102lb) bomb

SEAPLANES AND MARITIME AIRCRAFT

Arado Ar 196

Germany's principal floatplane of World War II, the Arado Ar 196 resulted from a specification issued in 1936 by the *Technische Amt* (Technical Department) of the *Reichsluftfahrtministerium* (German Air Ministry).

Arado Ar 196A-3
Part of 1./Bordfliegergruppe 196, Ar 196A-3 T3+BL was shore-based at Wilhelmshaven in 1940, but went to sea aboard the battleship *Tirpitz* operating around Norway in April 1942.

Arado Ar 196A-3
Weight (Maximum take-off) 3720kg (8201lb)
Dimensions Length: 11m (36ft 8in), Wingspan: 12.4m (40ft 8in), Height: 4.45m (14ft 7in)
Powerplant One 708kW (950hp) BMW 132K nine-cylinder radial piston engine
Speed 311km/h (193mph)
Range 1080km (670 miles)
Ceiling 7010m (23,000ft)
Crew 2
Armament One 7.92mm (0.31in) MG 15 machine gun (nose), one 7.92mm (0.31in) MG 17 machine gun (rear cockpit), two 20mm (0.8in) MG FF cannon (wings); two 50kg (110lb) bombs

The Air Ministry needed a catapult-equipped aircraft to replace Heinkel He 50s then serving with the *Bordfliegerstaffeln* – the Luftwaffe units responsible for operating spotter aircraft from capital ships and other surface vessels. The requirement called for a two-seat single- or twin-float aircraft with a powerplant developing between 597 and 671kW (800 and 900hp).

The Ar 196 faced competition from the Focke-Wulf Fw 62 biplane but was a more modern proposition. It was a monoplane configuration and all-metal construction, with a rectangular-section steel-tube fuselage frame that was faired to an oval cross-section using formers and stringers. The fuselage featured metal skinning forward and fabric covering aft. The wings were metal-skinned two-spar structures that were hinged at the trailing edges to fold back along the fuselage sides for stowage. Prior to wing-fold, the outboard wing-to-float struts were detached at the float end. Each of the twin floats contained a 300-litre (66-Imp gal) fuel tank.

Test flights
After evaluation of two Ar 196A prototypes powered by the 656kW (880hp) BMW 132De engine at Travemünde in summer 1937, the Arado design proved successful and another two prototypes were ordered; these were completed to the Ar 196B standard that featured single central/twin outboard stabilizing floats rather than the twin main floats of the Ar 196A. A fifth prototype Ar 196B introduced a new powerplant in the form of the 708kW (950hp) BMW 132K engine driving a three- (rather than two-) blade propeller.

Although there was little difference in performance between the different float configurations, the twin-float arrangement of the Ar 196A was

SEAPLANES AND MARITIME AIRCRAFT

Arado Ar 196A-5
An Ar 196A-5 from 4./Seeaufklärungsgruppe 126 that operated from Vukovar, Croatia, in January 1944.

selected for the pre-production Ar 196A-0, 10 of which were ordered.

The initial series-production model was the Ar 196A-1, which first went to sea aboard the pocket battleship *Admiral Graf Spee*, which was scuttled off Montevideo in December 1939. Other major warships on which this version served included *Deutschland*, *Scharnhorst*, *Gneisenau*, *Admiral Scheer* and *Prinz Eugen*.

After 20 of the Ar 196A-1 variant had been built, production switched to the Ar 196A-2 with armament increased by the addition of two 20mm (0.8in) MG FF wing cannons and a forward fuselage 7.92mm (0.31in) MG 17 machine gun.

The Ar 196A-3 incorporated further improvements, including structural strengthening and additional radio equipment and a new three-blade variable-pitch propeller. The Ar 196A-4 was another catapult version that replaced the Ar 196A-1 within the Kriegsmarine-controlled *Bordfliegerstaffeln*.

Arado Ar 196A-5
Weight (Maximum take-off) 3720kg (8201lb)
Dimensions Length: 11m (36ft 1in), Wingspan: 12.4m (40ft 8in), Height: 4.45m (14ft 7in)
Powerplant One 706kW (947hp) BMW 132K nine-cylinder radial piston engine
Speed 311km/h (193mph)
Range 1080km (670 miles)
Ceiling 7010m (23,000ft)
Crew 2
Armament One 7.92mm (0.31in) MG 17 machine gun (nose), two 8mm (0.32in) MG 81Z machine guns (rear cockpit), two 20mm (0.8in) MG FF cannon (wings); two 50kg (110lb) bombs

An Ar 196 passes a German destroyer in the Adriatic Sea in 1943. This Arado Ar 196A-3 belonged to 4./Bordfliegergruppe 196.

The last of the production versions was the Ar 196A-5, with further improved radios and twin 7.92mm (0.31in) MG 81Z machine guns in the rear cockpit.

Ultimately, production extended to more than 500 aircraft, including examples of the Ar 196A-3 built by SNCA at Saint-Nazaire in France and by Fokker in Amsterdam. The latter factory was responsible for the final deliveries of the Ar 196A-5 variant, completed in August 1944. The Ar 196 served in most major theatres and also equipped the Bulgarian and Romanian air forces.

Dornier Do 26

Developed as a transatlantic mailplane, the four-engine Dornier Do 26 was aerodynamically the cleanest of the company's long line of flying boats, doing away with the traditional parasol wing and sponsons.

The all-metal aircraft was intended to carry a crew of four and 500kg (1102lb) of mail between Lisbon and New York. It featured mid-span stabilizing floats that retracted completely into the wings. The Junkers Jumo 205 diesel engines were arranged as two tandem pairs, the rear pair of which could be tilted upwards by 10 degrees so that the metal three-blade propellers were clear of spray from the hull on take-off.

Do 26A

Deutsche Lufthansa ordered three catapult-equipped Do 26s in 1937 and the first took to the air in May the following year. Two were completed before the outbreak of the war and delivered to the airline as Do 26A aircraft, employed on South Atlantic routes.

Do 26D

The Do 26B designation covered the third aircraft, intended to have been completed with an enlarged cabin for four passengers, but which eventually became the first Do 26D.

The four D-series aircraft completed for the Luftwaffe were powered by 522kW (700hp) Jumo 205Ea engines and armed with three 7.92mm (0.31in) MG 15 machine guns and a single 20mm (0.8in) MG 151/20 cannon in a bow turret.

By April 1940, these four aircraft had been joined by the three Lufthansa machines, each carrying up to 12 fully equipped troops in support of the campaign in Norway. The Do 26Ds later served with the *Transozean Staffel* and subsequently with Küstenfliegergruppe 406.

Dornier Do 26 V4

Operating in Norway in 1940 as P5+DF, this is the fourth prototype, Do 26 V4, that was first flown in January that year. It formed part of the Transozeanstaffel incorporated in 9./Kampfgeschwader zur besonderen Verwendung 108 (9./KGzbV 108).

Dornier Do 26 V4
Weight (Maximum take-off) 8837kg (19,482lb)
Dimensions Length: 15.8m (51ft 10in), Wingspan: 18m (59ft 1in), Height: 4.56m (15ft)
Powerplant Two 522kW (700hp) Jumo 205Ea piston engines
Speed 350km/h (220mph)
Range 660km (410 miles)
Ceiling 8200m (26,900ft)
Crew 1
Armament Three 7.92mm (0.31in) MG 15 machine guns, one 20mm (0.8in) MG 151/20 cannon

SEAPLANES AND MARITIME AIRCRAFT

Fieseler Fi 167

Developed as a two-seat torpedo-bomber/reconnaissance aircraft, the Fieseler Fi 167 was intended for service aboard the aircraft carrier *Graf Zeppelin*, launched in December 1938.

The aircraft faced competition from the Arado Ar 195, but trials of prototypes of both revealed the superiority of the Fieseler design.

The Fi 167 was a two-bay foldable-wing biplane of mainly metal construction with some fabric covering. The fixed tailwheel landing gear incorporated jettisonable main units, while the tail unit was of the conventional braced type; power was provided by a Daimler-Benz DB 601 engine. Both wings featured ailerons and full-span automatic leading-edge slats, with large-area trailing-edge flaps on the lower wing conferring excellent low-speed manoeuvrability. The crew of two was seated in tandem beneath a long canopy with provision for a defensive machine gun operated by the back-seater.

The initial prototype, the Fi 167 V1, was followed by a second, Fi 167 V2, and then a pre-production batch of 12 Fi 167A-1 aircraft. These pre-production machines differed only in detail from the prototypes, taking into account initial testing and adding a two-man dinghy.

Fieseler Fi 167A-0
Fi 167A-0 TJ+AN as it appeared when operated by the Erprobungsstaffel 167, based in the Netherlands in 1940.

Cancelled order

When construction of the *Graf Zeppelin* was abandoned in 1940, the role of the Fi 167 no longer existed. Further work on the carrier was eventually authorized in 1942, but by this stage it had been decided that a navalized version of the Junkers Ju 87 would fulfil the carrier-based torpedo-bomber/reconnaissance role. The remaining Fi 167s were instead used for experimental duties in the Netherlands, nine examples eventually being sold to Romania.

Fieseler Fi 167A-0
Weight (Maximum take-off) 4859kg (10,712lb)
Dimensions Length: 11.4m (37ft 5in), Wingspan: 13.5m (44ft 3in), Height: 4.8m (5ft 9in)
Powerplant One 820kW (1100hp) Daimler-Benz DB 601B V-12 piston engine
Speed 325km/h (202mph)
Range 1300km (810 miles)
Ceiling 8200m (26,900ft)
Crew 2
Armament One 7.92mm (0.31in) MG 17 and one 7.92mm (0.31in) MG 15 machine gun; one 1000kg (2200lb) SC1000 bomb or one 765kg (1687lb) LT F5b torpedo or one 500kg (1100lb) SC500 bomb plus four 50kg (110lb) SC50 bombs

Blohm und Voss BV 138

The origins of the BV 138 can be traced back to the Ha 138 – the first flying boat design from the Hamburger Flugzeugbau GmbH, designed under the leadership of Richard Vogt.

The Ha 138 had in turn been preceded by the Ha 135 two-seat biplane, the Ha 136 single-seat monoplane and the Ha 137 dive-bomber. An initial three prototypes of the twin-engine Ha 138 flying boat were constructed, with plans for each to be powered by a different powerplant, for evaluation. Engines with an output of 746kW (1000hp) were specified.

In the event, development delays meant that the basic design had to be reconfigured for a three-engine powerplant, in the form of a trio of 485kW (650hp) Junkers Jumo 205C engines.

Initial prototype

Around two years after a first mock-up had been completed, the initial prototype Ha 138 V1 took off for its maiden flight on 15 July 1937. The second prototype, Ha 138 V2, introduced a revised hull form and began trials at Travemünde in November 1937. The first two aircraft were soon revealed to suffer from instability, both in the air and on water. Despite a modification of the vertical tail surfaces, the aircraft's handling was not greatly improved. Instead, the design team returned to work and undertook a complete revision of the aircraft, producing the BV 138 (its designation now reflecting the name of the Blohm und Voss company, of which Hamburger Flugzeugbau was a division).

Compared to its predecessor, the BV 138 featured a much-enlarged hull, with improved planning surfaces. Meanwhile, the revised tail surfaces were now mounted on more substantial horizontal booms. The initial prototype BV 138A was followed by five pre-production BV 138A-0 machines, before the aircraft entered series production for the Luftwaffe as the BV 138A-1.

Blohm und Voss BV 138C-1
A BV 138C of 1./ Seeaufklärungsgruppe 130, operating in Norway in 1943.

Blohm und Voss BV 138C-1
Weight (Maximum take-off) 17,650kg (38,967lb)
Dimensions Length: 19.85m (65ft 1in), Wingspan: 26.94m (88ft 5in), Height: 5.9m (19ft 4in)
Powerplant Three 656kW (880hp) Junkers Jumo 205D six-cylinder diesel engines
Speed 285km/h (177mph)
Range 1220km (760 miles)
Ceiling 5000m (16,000ft)
Crew 6
Armament Two 20mm (0.8in) MG 151 cannons (nose turret and rear fuselage), one 13mm (0.51in) MG 131 machine gun (behind centre engine nacelle), one to three 7.92mm (0.31in) MG 15 machine guns (optional); up to six 50kg (110lb) bombs or four 150kg (330lb) depth charges (optional)

SEAPLANES AND MARITIME AIRCRAFT

BV 138A-1
The initial production BV 138A-1 that first flew in April 1940 was available to the Luftwaffe in time for the Norwegian campaign of that year, during which it served with maritime reconnaissance units. Only built in modest numbers, the BV 138A-1 was armed with a single 20mm (0.8in) cannon in a bow turret and a pair of 7.92mm (0.31in) MG 17 machine guns, one in each of two uncovered positions, located behind the centre engine nacelle and at the rear of the hull. Once in service, the A-series began to show a number of limitations, including problems with the structure, engines and bow armament.

BV 138B series
After 25 examples of the BV 138A-1 had been built, production switched to the BV 138B series. The first of the B-series, the prototype BV 138B-0 (previously the BV 138A-04, the fourth pre-production A-series aircraft), was powered by three 656kW (880hp) Jumo 205D engines and had a reconfigured armament comprising one 20mm (0.8in) MG 151/20 cannon in the bow turret and a similar weapon in the rear hull position. Standard disposable

Blohm und Voss BV 138MS
Equipped for mine warfare, this BV 138MS was on strength with 1. Minensuchstaffel, part of Minensuchgruppe 1, operating along the Baltic Coast in 1944.

stores comprised up to 150kg (331lb) of ordnance carried beneath the starboard wing root.

Beginning in late 1940, a total of 19 production BV 138B-1 aircraft were built, to which were added 10 pre-series BV 138B-0 aircraft. The BV 138B-1/U1 factory conversion increased the weapon load to six 50kg (110lb) bombs or four 150kg (330lb) depth charges.

New C-series
The C-series that appeared in March 1941 introduced a new powerplant in the form of three Jumo 205D engines as well as further structural strengthening. In the production BV 138C-1 the central engine was equipped with a four-blade propeller (retrofitted to the previous BV 138B-1 aircraft). Although the outer pair of engines retained the previous three-blade units, these blades were now of broader chord. As well as the armament of the BV 138B-1, the C-1 added a 13mm (0.51in) MG 131

Blohm und Voss BV 138MS
Weight (Maximum take-off) 17,650kg (38,967lb)
Dimensions Length: 19.85m (65ft 1in), Wingspan: 26.94m (88ft 5in), Height: 5.9m (19ft 4in)
Powerplant Three 656kW (880hp) Junkers Jumo 205D six-cylinder diesel engines
Speed 285km/h (177mph)
Range 1220km (760 miles)
Ceiling 5000m (16,000ft)
Crew 6
Armament N/A

cannon in a position behind the centre engine nacelle.

The previous five-man crew was increased to six in the C-series and some of these aircraft were additionally equipped with FuG 200 Hohentwiel radar for maritime surveillance. The BV 138C-1 became the most important version, with a run of 279 examples from the total production figure of 279 of all variants that were built between 1939 and 1943. The BV 138C-1/U1 factory conversion also included the additional armament capability; all aircraft could also be be fitted with rocket-assisted take-off gear.

One unusual development of the flying boat was the BV 138MS for the minesweeping mission. Based on the airframe of BV 138B-0 pre-production aircraft, the BV 138MS had its armament removed and a degaussing loop of duralumin running around the airframe; this was provided with field-generating equipment to detonate mines below the aircraft. A handful of these conversions were completed during 1942–43.

This Blohm und Voss BV 138C-1 is flying off the coast of the Black Sea in southern Russia. It was based at Constanta, Romania, with 3.(F)/SAGr 125.

SEAPLANES AND MARITIME AIRCRAFT

Blohm und Voss BV 222

The largest flying boat to attain operational status during World War II, the BV 222 *Wiking* ('Viking') was an original design from the prolific Richard Vogt and his chief of aerodynamics and hydrodynamics at Hamburger Flugzeugbau, Richard Schubert.

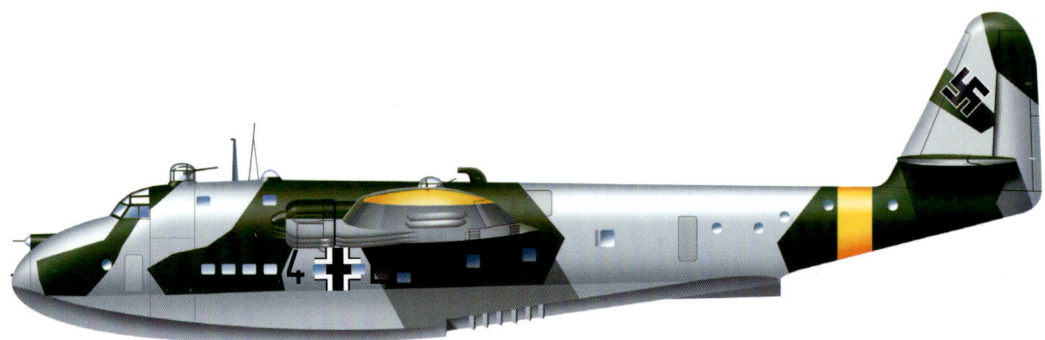

Initially schemed as a civilian project to meet a Lufthansa requirement of 1937 for a long-range passenger transport, it was envisaged that the resulting flying boat would carry 16 passengers between Berlin and New York in a flight time of 20 hours; for shorter-haul routes, passenger accommodation would be increased to 24.

In September 1937, an order was placed for three prototype aircraft, each of which would be powered by six BMW-Bramo Fafnir 323R radial engines, each developing 746kW (1000hp). Work on the first of these aircraft began in January the following year. The resulting aircraft was based around a capacious fuselage, with an almost 3.05m (10ft) beam yielding a large and unobstructed floor area. A tubular main spar for the wing also provided space for fuel and oil tanks, while the outboard stabilizing floats each split into halves and retracted sideways into the wing.

A first flight was completed by the initial prototype on 7 September

Blohm und Voss BV 222A-0 (V5) Wiking
This BV 222A-0 (the fifth prototype, or V5) was on the strength of Lufttransportstaffel (See) 222, flying from Petsamo, Finland, in early 1943.

1940 under the command of test pilot Helmut Rodig. By now the type's military potential was recognized and the first prototype was soon fitted with enlarged doors for Luftwaffe transport duty; in this form, an initial operational sortie was flown on 10 July 1941. Following a period of service in Norway, the flying boat was transferred to the Mediterranean theatre, where it ferried supplies to German forces in North Africa.

New defensive armament
Taking to the air on 7 August and 28 November 1941, respectively, the second and third prototypes introduced defensive armament. While the third prototype was armed with only a single 7.92mm (0.3in) machine gun in the bow, the second was fitted with additional weapons of similar

Blohm und Voss BV 222A-0 (V5) Wiking
Weight (Maximum take-off) 50,000kg (110,231lb)
Dimensions Length: 37m (121ft 5in), Wingspan: 46m (150ft 11in), Height: 10.9m (35ft 9in)
Powerplant Six 745kW (1000hp) Junkers Jumo 207C 12-cylinder diesel engines
Speed 390km/h (242mph)
Range 6100km (3790 miles)
Ceiling 7300m (23,950ft)
Crew 11–14
Armament One 7.92mm (0.31in) MG 81 machine gun (hull), two 13mm (0.51in) MG 131 (turret) and two 20mm (0.8in) MG 151 machine guns (wing turrets)

calibre in each of four waist positions and in two upper turrets, plus a pair of 13mm (0.51in) MG 131 machine guns in two gondolas located beneath the centre section. The bow and waist armament was then retrofitted to the first prototype, which also received an MG 131 in each of the upper turrets.

In this form, the first prototype was the first to be delivered to a frontline unit when it was handed over to Lufttransportstaffel (See) 222. The second prototype joined the same unit in August 1942, after it had been fitted with a modified planning hull to improve its handling on water. This work was undertaken following a period of evaluation at Travemünde.

The initial three prototypes were followed by another four BV 222A aircraft, completed to a similar standard for service with the Luftwaffe; they could carry either 76 troops or an equivalent load of freight.

Maritime reconnaissance role

By the end of 1942 it had been decided to switch the *Wiking* from the transport role to maritime reconnaissance and the operating unit was accordingly re-designated as the Aufklärungsstaffel (See) 222; subsequently, another unit was created with the same task: 1.(Fern)/Seeaufklärungsgruppe 129 based at Biscarrosse, France.

A total of four aircraft were adapted for the new mission, receiving FuG 200 Hohentwiel surveillance radar and revised armament: three power-operated dorsal turrets and two more at quarter-span positions above the wings.

BV 222C

Subsequent production encompassed the BV 222C version, of which five examples were completed and flown. They were preceded by a single development aircraft – the seventh prototype, modified – that took to the air on 1 April 1943. The BV 222C was powered by three Jumo 207C diesel engines, each rated at 731kW (980hp); armament was further boosted with additional machine guns in the nose and sides of the hull.

Blohm und Voss BV 222 V10 (C-10) Wiking

The tenth prototype, BV 222 V10 (C-10), equipped with Jumo 207C diesel engines, was assigned to the Fliegerführer Atlantik in July 1943. It crashed in February the following year.

Blohm und Voss BV 222 V10 (C-10) Wiking
Weight (Maximum take-off) 45,900kg (101,391lb)
Dimensions Length: 37m (121ft 5in), Wingspan: 46m (150ft 11in), Height: 11.90m (39ft)
Powerplant Six 731kW (980hp) Junkers Jumo 207C six-cylinder diesel engines
Speed 343km/h (23mph)
Range 6000km (3730 miles)
Ceiling 7300m (24,000ft)
Crew 11–14
Armament Five 13mm (0.51in) MG 131 machine guns (one in nose and four in beam positions) and three 20mm (0.8in) MG 151 machine guns (one each in forward turret and two wing turrets)

SEAPLANES AND MARITIME AIRCRAFT

Heinkel He 114

The Heinkel He 114 was developed as a successor to the He 60 for catapult launch from warships and was initially schemed as a private venture.

A total of five prototypes were flown between 1936 and 1937, powered by a range of different engines, including the 716kW (960hp) Daimler-Benz DB 600, the 477kW (640hp) Junkers Jumo 210, the 656kW (880hp) BMW 132Dc and the 716kW (960hp) BMW 132K.

Ten pre-production He 114A-0 aircraft were completed with the BMW 132Dc engine, the same unit also powering the 33 He 114A-1 aircraft that were completed as trainers. After the BMW 132K was evaluated in a test flown in February 1937, this engine was selected for the subsequent He 114A-2, the first operational version, armed with a fixed forward-firing 7.92mm (0.31in) MG 17 machine gun, with a similar weapon mounted in the observer's cockpit.

The He 114 was also produced for export, including 14 He 114A-2s completed for Sweden under the He 114B-1 designation, and six He 114B-2 aircraft for Romania. Of the initial Romanian aircraft, three were powered by DB 600 engines and three by Jumo 210s. Romania also received 12 He 114B-2 aircraft powered by the BMW 132K.

He 114C-1

The Luftwaffe's C-series included 14 He 114C-1 aircraft armed with an additional 7.92mm (0.31in) MG 17; some aircraft were also fitted with up to four 50kg (110lb) bombs. Production ended in 1939 and the type saw limited wartime use, in particular among units stationed in the Mediterranean, where the He 114 was still active in 1941–42.

Heinkel He 114C-1

This Heinkel He 114C-1 was active with 1./Seeaufklärungsgruppe 125 in the Baltic area in 1941.

Heinkel He 114C-1

Weight (Maximum take-off) 3670kg (8091lb)
Dimensions Length: 11.65m (38ft 3in), Wingspan: 13.6m (44ft 7in), Height: 5.23m (17ft 2in)
Powerplant One 716kW (960hp) BMW 132 nine-cylinder radial piston engine
Speed 335km/h (208mph)
Range 920km (570 miles)
Ceiling 4900m (16,100ft)
Crew 2
Armament Two 7.92mm (0.31in) MG 17 machine guns (fixed forward-firing and cockpit); two or four 50kg (110lb) bombs

Heinkel He 115

The Heinkel He 115 floatplane was conceived as a replacement for the He 59 and first took to the air in prototype form in 1936.

After its two machine guns were removed and their positions faired over, the same aircraft was prepared for a series of record attempts, securing eight payload/speed records on 30 March 1938.

The second prototype was little different to the first, while the third introduced the 'glasshouse' canopy that went on to be standard. The fourth aircraft served as the production prototype and had the float/fuselage bracing wires replaced by struts.

A- and B-series

A total of 10 pre-production He 115A-0 aircraft were manufactured in 1937 and were armed with a single machine gun. The He 115A-1 was the initial-production variant that added a nose-mounted machine gun. The similar He 115A-2 was exported to Norway and Sweden. The first model to see quantity production for the Luftwaffe was the He 115A-3 that had a modified bomb bay and changes to the radio fit. The first Luftwaffe unit to receive the He 115 was 1./Küstenfliegergruppe 106,

Heinkel He 115B-1
Based in France in 1942, this He 115B-1 flew with 1./Küstenfliegergruppe 706.

which began to accept its aircraft at the outbreak of the war.

The B-series was launched by the He 115B-1 with increased fuel capacity and the He 115B-2, which was fitted with reinforced floats for operations from snow or ice. All of the B-series aircraft were also to carry a single 1000kg (2205lb) magnetic mine, with a commensurate reduction in fuel and/or standard bomb load. By this stage, all aircraft production was being handled by the Weser Flugzeugbau company, output from Heinkel's Marienehe plant having been terminated after the 62nd production aircraft.

He 115C series

The He 115C series appeared in 1941 and included the He 115C-1 with additional armament in the form of one fixed forward-firing 15mm (0.59in) MG 151 cannon in the lower

Heinkel He 115B-1
Weight (Maximum take-off) 10,400kg (22,928lb)
Dimensions Length: 17.3m (56ft 9in), Wingspan: 22.2m (73ft 1in), Height: 6.6m (21ft 8in)
Powerplant Two 710kW (950hp) BMW 132K nine-cylinder radial piston engines
Speed 327km/h (203mph)
Range 2100km (1300 miles)
Ceiling 5200m (17,100ft)
Crew 3
Armament One 7.92mm (0.31in) MG 17 machine gun (nose), one 7.92mm (0.31in) MG 15 machine gun (rear cockpit); one 1000kg (2205lb) sea mine

SEAPLANES AND MARITIME AIRCRAFT

port side of the nose, one 7.92mm (0.31in) MG 17 fixed rearward-firing machine gun in the rear of each engine nacelle, one 7.92mm (0.31in) MG 15 trainable forward-firing machine gun in the nose position and one MG 15 trainable rearward-firing machine gun in the dorsal position. The aircraft could also take up to 1000kg (2205lb) of disposable stores carried in a lower-fuselage weapons bay and on two hardpoints under the wings. Meanwhile, the He 115C-2 had the same reinforced floats as the 115B-2. The He 115C-3 and He 115C-4 were equipped for minelaying and torpedo-carrying, respectively.

The He 115D designation applied to a single He 115A-1 airframe that was fitted with two 1193kW (1600hp) BMW 801C engines.

New production

The production line was reopened in 1941 to produce the He 115E series, which yielded the He 115E-1 that was similar to the He 115C but with a revised armament fit.

The He 115 saw wartime service with Luftwaffe coastal reconnaissance units and at the outbreak examples were also used to deliver parachute

Heinkel He 115C-1

This He 115C-1 was part of the inventory of 1./Küstenfliegergruppe 106, operating in Norway in 1941.

mines in British waters. Following the German invasion, three of the six Norwegian He 115A-2 aircraft (plus one captured German example) arrived in the UK and were later pressed into use on clandestine missions flown in both Norway and the Mediterranean.

The Heinkel He 115C-1 was heavily armed, with four machine guns providing protection as well as the ability to hit enemy targets.

Heinkel He 115C-1

Weight (Maximum take-off) 10,400kg (22,928lb)
Dimensions Length: 17.3m (56ft 9in), Wingspan: 22.3m (73ft 1in), Height: 6.6m (21ft 8in)
Powerplant Two 710kW (950hp) BMW 132K nine-cylinder radial piston engines
Speed 327km/h (203mph)
Range 2100km (1300 miles)
Ceiling 5200m (17,100ft)
Crew 3
Armament One 15mm (0.59in) MG 151 cannon (glazed nose), one 7.92mm (0.31in) MG 15 forward-firing machine gun (nose), two 7.92mm (0.31in) MG 17 fixed rearward-firing machine guns (rear of each engine nacelle), one MG 15 rearward-firing machine gun (dorsal position); 1000kg (2205lb) disposable stores

Blohm und Voss BV 238

The remarkable BV 238 was the heaviest aircraft ever built when it first flew in 1944, and was the largest aircraft produced by any of the Axis powers during World War II.

In early 1940, Richard Vogt began design work on a very large long-range flying boat for Lufthansa service. The project was shelved in early 1941 when the Blohm und Voss company received a German Air Ministry request for a multi-purpose long-range flying boat for military use.

Prototypes
A total of four protypes of the resulting BV 238 were ordered. These were to be completed as three BV 238A aircraft and a single BV 238B. All were to be powered by six engines; however, while the A-series used a liquid-cooled powerplant, the B-series was to make use of air-cooled engines.

Scale model
Such was the size of the aircraft that a roughly quarter-scale research aircraft was built for the initial test programme. Again powered by six engines, this was the FGP 227 that was completed in Prague. In the event, it was wasted effort, since this scale-model didn't take to the air until a few months before the full-scale machine.

The BV 238 was of similar configuration to the BV 222, but featured a high-mounted rather than a shoulder-mounted wing, a modified tail unit and one-piece (rather than split) retractable stabilizing floats.

First flight
The initial prototype BV 238 V1 took to the air for the first time in spring 1945, but was destroyed in a strafing attack on Lake Schaal in northern Germany by US Army Air Force (USAAF) P-51 Mustang fighters a few days before the end of the war.

Blohm und Voss BV 238V-1
Only one prototype BV 238 was completed and began trials in April 1944. It was partially sunk by Allied fighters four days before the war's end while moored at Lake Schaal, Germany.

Blohm und Voss BV 238V-1
Weight (Maximum take-off) 85,000kg (187,393lb)
Dimensions Length: 43.36m (142ft 3in), Wingspan: 60.2m (197ft 5in), Height: 13.4m (44ft)
Powerplant Six 1305kW (1750hp) Daimler-Benz DB 603 V-12 engines
Speed 446km/h (277mph)
Range 7200km (4474 miles)
Ceiling 7300m (23,950ft)
Crew 12
Armament 20 13mm (0.51in) MG 131 machine guns, two 20mm (0.8in) MG 151 cannon; 20 250kg (551lb) SC 250 bombs and four 1000kg (2205lb) SC 1000 bombs or two 1200kg (2646lb) LD 1200 torpedoes or four Henschel Hs 293 missiles or two 1000kg (2205lb) BV 143 glide bombs

HELICOPTERS

The very first helicopters proved to be difficult to master, and although a first example was airborne in September 1907, it wasn't until Germany introduced the Flettner Fl 282 *Kolibri* that a truly useful rotorcraft reached the front line. Delivered to the German Navy from 1942, it was followed by the more capable Focke-Achgelis Fa 223 *Drache*, a six-seater with options for various defensive weapons, but the helicopter as a weapon was still immature by the time World War II ended.

This chapter includes the following helicopters:

- Flettner Fl 265
- Flettner Fl 282 *Kolibri*
- Focke-Achgelis Fa 223 *Drache*
- Focke-Achgelis Fa 330 *Bachstelze*

A rare photograph of a Focke-Achgelis Fa 223 *Drache*, which had six seats.

HELICOPTERS

Flettner Fl 265

Rotary-wing aircraft pioneer Anton Flettner developed the two-seat Fl 184 autogyro powered by a 104kW (140hp) Siemens-Halske Sh 14 radial engine driving a tractor propeller, plus an auto-rotating three-blade rotor.

The aircraft was destroyed before evaluation could commence but it was followed by the Fl 185 autogyro/helicopter, in which a similar engine drove not only the main rotor but also two variable-pitch propellers mounted on outriggers, one on each side of the fuselage. Once selected for helicopter mode, the outrigger propellers were set so one acted as a tractor and the other as a pusher, offsetting main rotor torque. When operating as an autogyro, the outrigger propellers were both set to act as pushers and the main rotor was left to auto-rotate.

This concept paved the way for the further refined Fl 265, construction of which began in 1937. This utilized the same basic airframe design as the Fl 185, with a radial piston engine in the nose, but the previous variable-pitch propellers were deleted. Instead, it became a true helicopter. Power was supplied to two intermeshing and synchronized main rotors, which were counter-rotating to cancel out each other's torque.

The tail unit featured an adjustable tailplane for trimming and a large fin and rudder to supplement the differential collective-pitch change of the rotors in providing steering.

Active service

The first Fl 265 was lost in an accident when the rotors struck each other just three months after its first flight. The second prototype, the Fl 265 V2, was used for a variety of military trials. A total of six prototypes were built to meet a requirement of the German Navy and, although an order for quantity production followed in 1940, this was abandoned in favour of continued work on a more advanced Flettner design, the Fl 282 *Kolibri*.

Flettner Fl 265

The initial prototype, Fl 265 V1, registration D-EFLV, completed its maiden flight in May 1939 and subsequently undertook extensive military testing in conjunction with the Kriegsmarine before being removed from service in April 1940.

Flettner Fl 265

Weight (Maximum take-off) 1000kg (2205lb)
Dimensions Length: 6.16m (20ft 3in), Height: 2.82m (9ft 3in)
Powerplant One 119kW (160hp) BMW Bramo Sh.14A seven-cylinder radial piston engine
Speed 140km/h (87mph)
Range 300km (190 miles)
Ceiling 4100m (3500ft)
Crew 1
Armament N/A

Flettner Fl 282 *Kolibri*

The Fl 282 *Kolibri* ('hummingbird') was an improved development of the earlier Fl 265, and emerged as a two-seater primarily intended for naval use.

In early 1940, before it had even been tested, an order was placed for no fewer than 30 prototypes and 15 pre-production examples for use by the Kriegsmarine. The basic fuselage design was inherited from the Fl 265, but an important change was the introduction of a Bramo Sh 14A engine mounted in the centre fuselage, with the pilot seated in the nose.

A total of 24 prototypes were eventually built, these featuring different cockpit arrangements, including enclosed, semi-enclosed and fully open configurations. Some Fl 282s were also completed as single-seaters, while the two-seaters carried an observer in a position aft of the main rotor pylon, offering a good view to the rear of the aircraft.

Trials

German Navy trials of the *Kolibri* began in 1942 and the type proved to be very stable and highly manoeuvrable, with flying characteristics making it safe to fly in even poor weather conditions.

By the following year, around 20 of the 24 prototypes were operating on board warships in the Mediterranean and Aegean, mainly on convoy protection duties.

Production frustrated

The successful operational trials prompted an order for 1000 production examples, but these efforts were frustrated by the Allied bombing campaign targeting the BMW and Flettner factories responsible for the work. By the end of the war, only three of the prototypes survived, many more having been destroyed to prevent their capture.

Flettner Fl 282
CI+TU was the military identity of the Fl 282 V21, the 21st prototype, also known as the Fl 282B. It is shown as it appeared while undergoing evaluation in 1943.

Flettner Fl 282
Weight (Maximum take-off) 1000kg (2205lb)
Dimensions Length: 6.65m (21ft 10in), Height: 2.2m (7ft 3in)
Powerplant One 119Kw (160hp) Bramo Sh 14A seven-cylinder radial piston engine
Speed 150km/h (93mph)
Range 170km (106 miles)
Ceiling 3300m (10,827ft)
Crew 1
Armament Two 7.92mm (0.31in) WB 81 B MG 81 machine guns and four 88mm (3.5in) Panzerschreck anti-tank rocket launchers or eight Nebelhandgranate 39 grenades

HELICOPTERS

Focke-Achgelis Fa 223 *Drache*

The Focke-Achgelis company gained experience of a helicopter with an outrigger-mounted, twin-rotor arrangement with the Fa 61, which was then scaled up to create the six-passenger Fa 226 *Hornisse* ('hornet').

The latter was developed to meet a Deutsche Lufthansa requirement. The prototype completed ground-running and tethered-hovering trials in summer 1940 and a first free flight took place in August that year.

Further development continued under military jurisdiction as the Fa 223 *Drache* ('kite'), with an order placed for 39 examples for evaluation in roles including training, transport, rescue and anti-submarine patrol. Different equipment included a 7.92mm (0.31in) MG 15 machine gun and two 250kg (551lb) bombs, a camera for reconnaissance, or a jettisonable 300-litre (66-Imp gal) auxiliary fuel tank.

Production run

Ten of the planned 30 pre-production aircraft were completed in Bremen before the factory was bombed, and another seven were completed at Laupheim near Stuttgart. One more emerged from a factory in Berlin before the war came to an end. Most

Focke-Achgelis Fa 223
First flown in February 1945, the 51st prototype Fa 223 V23, received the military serial GW+PA. It was used for operational trials before it was captured by US troops.

of those completed didn't ever fly, but at least two entered service with Lufttransportstaffel 40, these being captured by US forces at Ainring, Austria, in May 1945.

Post-war development

One example became the first helicopter to cross the English Channel when it was transferred to the UK for evaluation in September 1945, although it was destroyed in an accident the following October.

Two more aircraft were completed in Czechoslovakia after the war using German-made components. Development also continued in post-war France, where the Sud Est SE 3000 first took to the air in October 1948.

Focke-Achgelis Fa 223
Weight (Maximum take-off) 4315kg (9513lb)
Dimensions Length: 12.25m (40ft 2in), Height: 4.36m (14ft 4in)
Powerplant One 750kW (1000hp) Bramo 323D-2 nine-cylinder radial engine
Speed 176km/h (109mph)
Range 437km (272 miles)
Ceiling 4875m (15,994ft)
Crew 2 + 4 passengers
Armament One 7.92mm (0.31in) MG 15 machine gun; 250kg (550lb) bombs or two depth charges

Focke-Achgelis Fa 330 *Bachstelze*

The Fa 330 *Bachstelze* ('white wagtail') was a single-seat rotary-wing observation kite, developed in order to provide U-boat commanders with an aerial surveillance capability.

The surveillance was designed to extend around 8km (5 miles) from the submarine, primarily to locate naval targets.

In 1942, Focke-Achgelis began work on a small, rotary-wing gyro-kite that could be launched, towed and retrieved from a submarine. This was intended to be quickly assembled and disassembled and featured a free-turning, three-blade rotor mounted on a pylon above a simple framework. The aircraft carried a pilot/observer and the tail unit was fitted with a tailplane, fin and rudder at the end of a braced tubular boom. Fa 330s were built by Weser Flugzeugbau, which produced around 200 examples.

Surface run

When employed operationally, the *Bachstelze*'s rotor was spun up manually before auto-rotating in the wind, with the U-boat running on the surface. The observation kite then flew at the end of a cable, towed along

Focke-Achgelis Fa 330
A type of rotary-wing kite – otherwise known as a gyroglider or rotor kite – the Fa 330 *Bachstelze* was towed behind German U-boats to allow a lookout to see farther.

by the submarine. The pilot/observer was provided with a telephone to communicate with the submarine, the cable extending to a length of 120m (394ft). At the end of the observation sortie, the aircraft would be winched back to the U-boat's deck.

Operational limitations

While the *Bachstelze* was able to extend the commander's situational awareness by a factor of five, in practice it was found to be hazardous to employ the observation kite, as the U-boat was no longer able to make an emergency dive. Their use was limited as a result, with most activity taking place in the South Atlantic and Indian Ocean, where the presence of Allied warships was less likely.

Focke-Achgelis Fa 330
Weight (Maximum take-off) 82kg (180lb)
Dimensions Length: 4.4m (14ft 6in), Height: 1.7m (5ft 6in)
Powerplant N/A
Speed 40km/h (25mph)
Crew 1
Armament N/A

Glossary

Aufklärung	Reconnaissance
Ausbildungs-	Training
Befehlshaber	Commander
Behelfs	Auxiliary
Beobachter	Observer/Navigator
Bodenlafette	Ventral gun mount
Bordkanone	Fixed aircraft cannon
Bordfliegerstaffel	Shipborne aircraft squadron
Bramo	Brandenburgische Motoren Werke
B-Schule	Advanced/Blind Flying Training School
B-Stand	Dorsal gunner's position
Buna	Synthetic rubber (originally a trade name)
C-Schule	Advanced Flying Training School, multi-engine
C-Stand	Ventral gunner's position
DFS	Deutsches Forschungsinstitut für Segelflug
Einsatzkommando	Combat Operations Detachment
EJG	Ergänzungs-Jagdgeschwader
EKdo	Erprobungs Kommando
Elektrische Trägervorrichtung	Electrically-operated bomb racks
Entwicklungs-	Development-
Ergänzungs-	Replacement-
Ergänzungs-Jagdgeschwader	Fighter Replacement Training Group
Ersatz	Substitute or Replacement
FA	Ferngesteuerte Anlage
FAGr	Fernaufklärungsgruppe
Fallschirmjäger	Paratroopers
Fernaufklärung	Long-range Reconnaissance
Fernaufklärungsgruppe	Long-range Reconnaissance Gruppe
Fernaufklärungsstaffel	Long-range reconnaissance Squadron
Fernnachtjagd	Long-range night fighter/intruder
Fernzielgerät	Remote aiming device or bombsight
FFS	Flugzeugführerschule
FHL	Ferngerichtete Hecklafette
Flak	Fliegerabwehrkanone
Flieger	Pilot (as description) or Airman (as rank)
Fliegerabwehrkanone	Anti-Aircraft Gun/Artillery
Fliegerdivision	Air Division
Fliegerkorps	Air Corps
Flugberietschaft	Duty Flight attached to higher formations
Flugzeugführerschule	Pilot/Aircraft Commander School
FuG	Funkgerät
Funkgerät	Radio or Radar set
Führerkurierstaffel	Führer's courier squadron
Führungsstab	Operations Staff
General	Lieutenant General or Air Marshal
General der Jagdflieger	General of Fighters
General der Kampfflieger	General of Bombers
Generalfeldmarschall	General of the Air Force/Marshal of the RAF
Generalleutnant	Major-General/Air Vice Marshal
Generalmajor	Brigadier-General/Air Commodore
Generaloberst	General/Air Chief Marshal
Geschwader	Equivalent to Allied Group
Geschwaderkommodore	Geschwader commander
Gruppe	Equivalent to Allied Wing
Gruppenkommandeur	Group commander
Hauptmann	Captain/Flight Lieutenant
Heeres-	Army
Heeresaufklärungstaffel	Army or Tactical Reconnaissance Squadron
Himmelbet	'Heavenly Bed' – Night ground-controlled intercept zone
HWK	Helmuth Walter Werke
Jabo	Jagdbomber
Jabo-Rei	*Jagdbomber mit vergrosster reichweite*
Jagd-	Fighter (Hunt, Chase, Pursuit)
Jagdbomber	Fighter bomber
Jagdfliegerführer	Fighter Command
Jagdfliegerschule	Fighter Training School
Jafü	*Jagdfliegerführer*
Jagdgeschwader	Fighter Group
Jagdgruppe	Fighter Wing
Jagdstaffel	Fighter Squadron
JG	*Jagdgeschwader*
JGr	*Jagdgruppe*
JFS	*Jagdfliegerschule*
Jumo	Junkers Motoren Werke
Kampf	Battle (Bomber, when applied to aircraft)
Kampfbeobachter	Artillery Observer
Kampfgeschwader	Bomber Group
Kampfgeschwader zur	Special Duty/Transport Group
Kampfgruppe	Bomber Wing
Kdo	Kommando
Kette	Flight of three aircraft
KG	*Kampfgeschwader*
KGr	*Kampfgruppe*
KGzbV	*Kampfgeschwader zur besonderen Verwendung*
Koluft	*Kommander der Luftwaffe bei einen AOK*
Kommando	Detachment
Kü.Fl	Küsten Flieger
Küsten Flieger	Coastal Aviation
Langstrecken-	Long-range
Lastensiegler	Cargo glider
Lehr-	Instruction
Lehrgeschwader	Demonstration/Operational development Group
Luftflotte	Air Fleet
Lufttorpedo	Air-dropped Torpedo
Lufttransportstaffel	Air Transport Squadron

GLOSSARY

Luftwaffe	Air Force	*Schwarm*	Flight of four fighters
Luftwaffenführungsstab	Luftwaffe Operations Staff	*Schnellbomber*	Fast bomber
Luftwaffengeneralstab	Luftwaffe Air Staff	*Schräge Musik*	'Slanting' or 'Jazz Music' – cannon firing obliquely upwards
Major	Major/Squadron Leader	SD	Splitterbomb, Dickwand
Maschinengewehr	Machine Gun	Sd.Kdo	Special Detachment
Maschinenkanone	Machine Cannon	*Seeaufklärungsgruppe*	Maritime Reconnaissance Wing
MG	*Maschinengewehr*	*Seenotsdienst*	Air Sea Rescue Service
Minensuchgruppe	Minehunting/sweeping wing	*Seenotsstaffel*	Air Sea Rescue Squadron
Mistel	(Mistletoe) – combination aircraft	SG	*Schlachtgeschwader*
MK	*Maschinenkanone*	SKG	*Schnellkampfgeschwader*
MW 50	Methanol-water mix	*Sonder-*	Special purpose
		Spanner-Anlage	Early infra-red sensor system
Nachtjagd-	Night Fighter	S-Stoff	Rocket fuel (97% Nitric Acid, 3% Sulphuric Acid)
Nachtjagdgeschwader	Night Fighter Group		
Nachtschlacht-	Night Harassment	*Stab-*	Staff
Nachtschlachtgruppe	Night Harassment Wing	*Stabschwarm*	Staff flight in a *Gruppe*
NAGr	*Nahaufklärungsgruppe*	*Staffel*	Squadron
Nahaufklärungs-	Short-range reconnaissance	*Staffelkapitan*	Squadron commander
Nahaufklärungsgruppe	Short-range reconnaissance group	St.G	*Sturzkampfgeschwader*
NJG	*Nachtjagdgeschwader*	*Störkampfstaffel*	Night Harassment Squadron
NSGr	*Nachtschlachtgruppe*	*Stuka*	*Sturzkampfflugzeug*
		Sturm-	Assault
Ob.d.L	*Oberbefehlshaber der Luftwaffe*	*Sturmgruppe*	Assault Wing
Ob.d.M	*Oberbefehlshaber der Marine*	*Sturzkampfflugzeug*	Dive bomber
Oberbefehlshaber der Luftwaffe	Commander-in-Chief of the Luftwaffe	*Sturzkampfgeschwader*	Dive bomber Group
		Sturz-visier	Dive Bombing Sight
Oberbefehlshaber der Marine	Commander-in-Chief of the Navy	*Trägergeschwader*	Aircraft Carrier Group
Oberfeldwebel	Master Sergeant/Flight Sergeant	*Troika-schlepp*	Triple tow (of large gliders by three aircraft)
Oberkommando des Heeres	Army High Command		
Oberkommando der Luftwaffe	Air Force High Command	*Umbau*	Reconstruction
Oberkommando der Marine	Navy High Command	*Umrüst-Bausatz*	Factory conversion kit
Oberkommando der Wehrmacht	High Command of the Armed Forces	V	*Versuchs* (Experimental)
Oberleutnant	First Lieutenant/Flying Officer	*Verband*	Formation
Oberst	Colonel/Group Captain	*Verstellschraube*	Variable pitch propeller
Oberstleutnant	Lieutenant Colonel/Wing Commander	VS	*Verstellschraube*
OKH	*Oberkommando des Heeres*		
OKL	*Oberkommando der Luftwaffe*	*Werfer-Granate*	Grenade projector/rocket propelled shell
OKM	*Oberkommando der Marine*	*Wettererkundungsstaffel*	Meteorological squadron
OKW	*Oberkommando der Wehrmacht*	Wfr.Gr	*Werfer-Granate*
Rauchgerät	Rocket-booster unit	X-Gerät	Electronic blind-flying/bombing aid
R-Gerät	*Rauchgerät*		
Rotte	A flight of two aircraft	Y-Gerät	Electronic blind-flying/range-finding aid
R-Stoff	Rocket fuel (57% Monoxylidene, 43% triethylamine)		
Rüstatz	Field conversion kit	*Zwilling*	Twin or coupled
		Zerstörer	Destroyer, or heavy fighter
SAGr	*See-Aufklärungsgruppe*	*Zerstörergeschwader*	Heavy Fighter Group
Sanitätsstaffel	Air Ambulance Squadron	ZG	*Zerstörergeschwader*
Sch.G	*Schlachtgeschwader*		
Schlacht-	Close-support/Assault		
Schlachtgeschwader	Close Support Group		
Schlepp-	Towing		
Schnellkampfgeschwader	High-speed Bomber/Attack Group		

Index

Page numbers in **bold** refer to illustration captions.

1./Bordfliegergruppe 196 **103**
1.(Fern) Staffel/Aufklärungsgruppe 124 **44**
1.(Fern)/Seeaufklärungsgruppe 129 **111**
1.(Heeres-)/Aufklärungsgruppe 32 **66**
1./Kampfgeschwader 2 **22**
1./Kampfgeschwader 30 **29**
1./Kampfgeschwader 40 **98**, 98
1./Kampfgeschwader 40 IV Fliegerkorps 100
1./Kampfgeschwader 66 **35**
1./Küstenfliegergruppe 106 113, **114**
1./Küstenfliegergruppe 706 **113**
1.Minensuchstaffel **108**
1./Seeaufklärungsgruppe 125 **112**
1./Seeaufklärungsgruppe 126 **93**
1./Seeaufklärungsgruppe 130 **107**
1./Versuchsverband Oberbefehlhaber der Luftwaffe 49
2.(Fern)/Aufklärungsgruppe 123 **34**
2.(Heeres-)/Aufklärungsgruppe 14 **64**
2./Kampfgeschwader 3 **29**
2./Kampfgeschwader 100 **39**
2./Küstenfliegergruppe 106 **94**
2./Küstenfliegergruppe 906 **94**
2./Nachtschlachtgruppe 4 **89**
2./Seeaufklärungsgruppe 126 **89**
3./Aufklärungsgruppe Oberbehlshaber der Luftwaffe **23**
3.Aufklärungsstaffel 23
3.(Fern)/Aufklarungsgruppe Nacht **21**
3.(F)/Seeaufklärungsgruppe 125 **109**
3./Kampfgeschwader 2 **26**
3./Kampfgeschwader 200 **85**
3./Stukageschwader 5 **60**
4./Bordfliegergruppe 196 **104**
4./Schlachtgeschwader 1 69
4./Seeaufklärungsgruppe 126 **104**
5./Kampfgeschwader 1 **41**
5./Kampfgeschwader 100 **40**
5./Kampfgruppe 88 **56**
5./Lehrgeschwader 1 **32**
5.(Schl)/Lehrgeschwader 2 **55**
6./Kampfgeschwader 2 **21**
6./Stukageschwader 2 **60**
7. Staffel III./Kampfgeschwader 3 **20**
7./Kampfgeschwader 40 **99**
7.Seenotstaffel/SBK XI **96**
7./Stukageschwader 51 **57**
7./Stukageschwader 165 **54**
8./Kampfgeschwader 76 **48**
8./Schlachtgeschwader 1 **70**
9.(Heeres-)/Lehrgeschwader 2 **63**
9./Kampfgeschwader 44 **16**
9./Kampfgeschwader zur besonderen Verwendung 108 **105**
9. Staffel, II./Kampfgeschwader 30 **32**
10.(Panzerjäger)/Schlachtgeschwader 2 **62**
13./Seeaufklärungsgruppe 125 **102**
14.(Panzerjäger)/Schlachtgeschwader 9 **70**
I./Kampfgeschwader 200 **83**
I./Kustenfliegergruppe 906 **92**
I./Stukageschwader 2 **61**
II./Kampfgeschwader 40 25, **27**
II./Kampfgeschwader 53 **13**
II./Kampfgeschwader 153 20
III./Kampfgeschwader 3 **15**
III./Kampfgeschwader 26 **43**
III./Kampfgeschwader 40 **99**
III./Kampfgeschwader 153 20
III./Kampfgeschwader 155 20
III./Lehrgeschwader 1 **28**
IV./Kampfgeschwader 101 **36**
IV./Kampfgruppe zur besonderen Verwendung 1 **76**

A
Arado Ar 95 **102**
Arado Ar 196 **103–5**
 Ar 196A **103–4**
 Ar 196A-1 **104**
 Ar 196A-2 **104**
 Ar 196A-3 103, **104**
 Ar 196A-5 **104**, 105
 Ar 196B 103
Arado Ar 232 **84–5**
 Ar 232A-0 **85**
 Ar 232B-0 **85**
Arado Ar 234 *Blitz* **47–50**
 Ar 234B-1 47, **49**
 Ar 234B-2 48, **49**
 Ar 234B-3/N **49**
 Ar 234B-7 **49–50**
 Ar 234C-1 **50**
 Ar 234C-2 **50**
 Ar 234C-3 **50**
Ardennes offensive (1944) **49**
Aufklärungsgruppe
 Aufklärungsgruppe 14 **64**
 Aufklärungsgruppe 32 **66**
 Aufklärungsgruppe 123 **34**
 Aufklärungsgruppe 124 **44**
Aufklarungsgruppe Nacht **21**
Aufklärungsgruppe Oberbefehlshaber der Luftwaffe 24
Aufklärungsgruppe Oberbehlshaber der Luftwaffe **23**
Aufklärungsstaffel 23, 111

B
Battle of Britain (1940) 32, 61
Battle of France (1940) **57**
Baumbach, Major Werner **29**
Belgium
 DFS 230 81
 Henschel Hs 123 **54**
Blohm und Voss BV 138 **107–9**
 BV 138A-1 **107–8**
 BV 138B-1 **108**
 BV 138C-1 107, **108–9**
 BV 138MS 108, **109**
Blohm und Voss BV 141 **72–3**
 BV 141A-0 **73**
 BV 141B-0 **73**
 BV 141B-1 **73**
Blohm und Voss BV 222 **110–11**
 BV 222A-0 **110**
 BV 222C **111**
Blohm und Voss BV 238 **115**
 BV 238V-1 **115**
Blohm und Voss Ha 139 **97**
 Ha 139B **97**
 Ha 139B/MS **97**
 Ha 139V3/U1 **97**
Blume, Walter 47, **102**
Bordfliegergruppe 196 **103, 104**
Bordfliegerstaffeln 104
Britain, Battle of (1940)
 Junkers Ju 87 61
 Junkers Ju 88 32

INDEX

British strikes
   Heinkel He 111 15
   Heinkel He 177 39, 41
   Junkers Ju 88 **32**
   Junkers Ju 188 **46**

C

campaigns
   Ardennes offensive (1944) **49**
   Belgium 54, 81
   British strikes 15, **32**, 39, 41, **46**
   Denmark **40**, 46
   Eastern Front **13**, 16, **20, 21**, 29, 38, 41, **41**, 55, **55**, 56, **60**, 61, **61, 62**, 69, **77**, 81, 93
   France **12, 26**, 38, **39**, 49, 54, 58, 69, **82, 98**, 111, **113**
   Greece **22**, 61, 63, 81, 88, 93, **93**
   Italy **34**, 69, 78
   the Netherlands 15, **22, 24**, 106, **106**
   North Africa **33**, 57, **60**, **64**, 69, **70, 80**, 110
   Norway **11**, **29**, **34**, **44**, 46, **48, 92**, 97, 98, **99**, **103**, 105, **107**, 108, 110, 114
   Poland **21, 23**, 29, 54, 56–7, **69**
   Sicily **33**
   Ukraine **23**
   Yugoslavia **20**
Condor Legion 10, **11**, 17, 54, 56, **56**, 63, 92

D

Denmark
   Heinkel He 177 **40**
   Junkers Ju 188 **46**
DFS 230 81
   230A-1 81
   230A-2 81
   230B 81
   230B-1 81
   230B-2 81
Dornier Do 17 19–22
   Do 17E-1 19–20
   Do 17F-1 20
   Do 17K 20
   Do 17L 21
   Do 17M-1 21
   Do 17P-1 21
   Do 17S-0 21–2
   Do 17U 22

   Do 17Z-0 22
   Do 17Z-1 22
   Do 17Z-2 22
   Do 17Z-3 22
   Do 17Z-4 22
   Do 17Z-5 22
Dornier Do 18 94
   Do 18a 94
   Do 18D-1 94
   Do 18E 94
   Do 18F 94
   Do 18G-1 94
   Do 18L 94
   Do 18N-1 94
Dornier Do 24 95–6
   Do 24K-1 95
   Do 24K-2 95
   Do 24N-1 96
   Do 24T-1 96
   Do 24T-2 96
   Do 24T-3 96
Dornier Do 26 105
   Do 26A 105
   Do 26D 105
Dornier Do 215 22–3
   Do 215A-1 23
   Do 215B-1 23
   Do 215B-3 23
   Do 215B-4 23
Dornier Do 217 24–7
   Do 217A-0 24
   Do 217C 24
   Do 217E 24–5
   Do 217E-1 25
   Do 217E-2 24, 25
   Do 217E-3 25
   Do 217E-4 25
   Do 217E-5 25
   Do 217K-1 26
   Do 217K-2 26
   Do 217K-3 26
   Do 217K-5 26
   Do 217L 26
   Do 217M-1 26
   Do 217M-3 26–7
   Do 217M-11 27
   Do 217P-0 27
Dornier Do 317 27

E

Eastern Front
   DFS 230 81

   Dornier Do 17 **20, 21**
   Heinkel He 60 93
   Heinkel He 111 **13**, 16
   Heinkel He 177 41, **41**
   Henschel Hs 123 55, **55**
   Henschel Hs 129 69
   Junkers Ju 52 **77**
   Junkers Ju 87 56, **60**, 61, **61, 62**
   Junkers Ju 88 **29**
   Junkers Ju 88 *Mistel* bombers 38
Ergänzungsgruppe 85
Erprobungsstaffel 167 **106**

F

Fernaufklärungsgruppe 5 **82**
Fernaufklärungsstaffel 98
Fieseler Fi 103R *Reichenberg* 51
Fieseler Fi 156 *Storch* 64–6
   Fi 156A-0 64
   Fi 156A-1 65
   Fi 156C-1 66
   Fi 156C-2 66
   Fi 156C-3 66
   Fi 156C-5 66
   Fi 156D-1 66
Fieseler Fi 167 106
   Fi 167A-0 106
Fieseler, Gerhard 64
Flettner, Anton 118
Flettner Fl 265 118
Flettner Fl 282 *Kolibri* 119
Focke-Achgelis Fa 223 *Drache* 120
Focke-Achgelis Fa 330 *Bachstelze* 121
Focke-Wulf Fw 189 *Uhu* 67–9
   Fw 189A-1 67, 69
   Fw 189A-2 67
   Fw 189A-4 68
   Fw 189B-0 68
   Fw 189B-1 68
   Fw 189C 68
   Fw 189F-1 69
   Fw 189F-2 69
Focke-Wulf Fw 200 *Kondor* 98–101
   Fw 200A 98
   Fw 200C-0 98
   Fw 200C-1 98, 100–1
   Fw 200C-2 98–9
   Fw 200C-3 98–9
   Fw 200C-4 99
   Fw 200C-6 99
   Fw 200C-8 99

INDEX

France
    Arado Ar 234 *Blitz* 49
    Blohm un Voss BV 222 111
    Dornier Do 217 **26**
    Focke-Wulf Fw 200 *Kondor* **98**
    Heinkel He 111 **12**
    Heinkel He 115 **113**
    Heinkel He 177 **39**
    Henschel Hs 123 54
    Henschel Hs 129 69
    Junkers Ju 87 58
    Junkers Ju 88 *Mistel* bombers 38
    Junkers Ju 290 **82**
France, Battle of (1940) **57**

G
Gotha Go 242 88
Gotha Go 244 88
Greece
    DFS 230 81
    Dornier Do 17 **22**
    Gotha 244 88
    Heinkel He 60 93, **93**
    Henschel Hs 126 63
    Junkers Ju 87 61
Greim, General Ritter von 66

H
Heinkel He 59 92
    He 59A 92
    He 59B-1 92
    He 59B-2 92
    He 59B-3 92
    He 59C-1 92
    He 59C-2 92
    He 59D-1 92
    He 59E-2 92
    He 59N 92
Heinkel He 60 93
    He 60A 93
    He 60B 93
    He 60B-3 93
    He 60D 93
    He 60E 93
Heinkel He 111 10–16
    He 111B-1 10–11
    He 111D 11
    He 111E-1 11
    He 111E-2 11
    He 111E-3 11
    He 111E-5 11
    He 111F-1 11
    He 111F-4 11
    He 111G-1 11
    He 111G-3 11
    He 111G-4 11
    He 111G-5 11–12
    He 111H-0 12
    He 111H-1 12
    He 111H-3 12–13
    He 111H-4 13
    He 111H-5 13
    He 111H-6 13
    He 111H-8 13
    He 111H-10 13
    He 111H-11 13
    He 111H-12 13
    He 111H-14 13
    He 111H-15 13
    He 111H-16 13, 16
    He 111H-18 16
    He 111H-20 16
    He 111H-21 16
    He 111H-22 14–15, 16
    He 111H-23 16
    He 111P-0 12
    He 111P-1 12
    He 111P-2 12
    He 111P-3 12
    He 111P-4 12
    He 111P-6 12
    He 111Z 16
Heinkel He 114 112
    He 114A-1 112
    He 114A-2 112
    He 114B-1 112
    He 114B-2 112
    He 114C-1 112
Heinkel He 115 113–14
    He 115A-1 113
    He 115A-2 113, 114
    He 115A-3 113
    He 115B-1 113
    He 115B-2 113
    He 115C-1 113–14
    He 115C-2 114
    He 115C-3 114
    He 115C-4 114
    He 115D 114
    He 115E-1 114
Heinkel He 177 39–41
    He 177A-1 39
    He 177A-3 39–40, 41
    He 177A-5 40, 41
    He 177A-6 40
    He 177A-7 41
Henschel Hs 123 54–5
    Hs 123A-1 54, 55
Henschel Hs 126 63–4
    Hs 126A-1 63, 64
    Hs 126B-1 63, 64
Henschel Hs 129 69–70
    Hs 129B-1 69, 70
    Hs 129B-2 69–70
    Hs 129B-3 69
Henschel Hs 132 71

I
Italy
    Henschel Hs 129 69
    Junkers Ju 52 78
    Junkers Ju 88 **34**

J
Junkers Ju 52 76–80
    Ju 52/3m 76
    Ju 52/3mg3e 76
    Ju 52/3mg4e 76–7
    Ju 52/3mg5e 77
    Ju 52/3mg6e 77
    Ju 52/3mg7e 77
    Ju 52/3mg8e 77
    Ju 52/3mg9e 77
    Ju 52/3mg10e 77
    Ju 52/3mg12e 77
    Ju 52/3mg14e 77
    Ju 52/3mge 76
Junkers Ju 86 17–18
    Ju 86A-1 17
    Ju 86B-0 17
    Ju 86C-1 17
    Ju 86D-1 17
    Ju 86E-1 17
    Ju 86E-2 18
    Ju 86G-1 18
    Ju 86K-1 17
    Ju 86K-2 17
    Ju 86K-6 17
    Ju 86K-13 17
    Ju 86P-1 18
    Ju 86P-2 18
Junkers Ju 87 56–62
    Ju 87A-1 56
    Ju 87A-2 56
    Ju 87B-1 56–7
    Ju 87B-2 56, 58–9

Ju 87D-1 60, 61
Ju 87D-3 60
Ju 87D-5 60–1
Ju 87D-7 61
Ju 87D-8 61
Ju 87G-1 61, 62
Ju 87G-2 62
Ju 87H 62
Junkers Ju 88 28–35
  Ju 88A-0 29, 32
  Ju 88A-1 29, 32
  Ju 88A-2 32
  Ju 88A-3 32
  Ju 88A-4 29
  Ju 88A-5 30–1, 32
  Ju 88A-6 33
  Ju 88A-9 33
  Ju 88A-10 33
  Ju 88A-11 33
  Ju 88A-14 33
  Ju 88A-17 34
  Ju 88D 33–4
  Ju 88G 34
  Ju 88H-1 34–5
  Ju 88H-2 34
  Ju 88P-1 34, 35
  Ju 88P-2 34
  Ju 88P-3 34
  Ju 88P-4 34
  Ju 88S-1 35
  Ju 88S-2 35
  Ju 88S-3 35
  Ju 88T 35
Junkers Ju 88 *Mistel* bombers 36–8
  Mistel 1 36
  Mistel 2 36, 37
  Mistel 3B 38
  Mistel 3C 38
Junkers Ju 188 43–6
  Ju 188A-2 45
  Ju 188A-3 43, 45
  Ju 188D-1 45
  Ju 188D-2 44, 45
  Ju 188E-1 44, 45
  Ju 188E-2 44, 46
  Ju 188F-1 45
  Ju 188F-2 45
  Ju 188G-0 45
  Ju 188G-2 45
  Ju 188S-1 46
  Ju 188T-1 46
Junkers Ju 290 82–3
  Ju 290A-1 82

Ju 290A-2 82
Ju 290A-3 82
Ju 290A-4 82–3
Ju 290A-5 83
Ju 290A-6 83
Ju 290A-7 83
Ju 290A-8 83
Ju 290A-9 83
Ju 290B-1 83

K
Kalkert, Albert 88
Kampfgeschwader
  Kampfgeschwader 1 **41**
  Kampfgeschwader 2 **21, 22, 26**
  Kampfgeschwader 3 15, **20, 29**
  Kampfgeschwader 6 **46**
  Kampfgeschwader 26 **11, 34, 43**
  Kampfgeschwader 30 29, **29**, 30, 32
  Kampfgeschwader 36 49
  Kampfgeschwader 40 25, **27**, 98, **98**, 99, **99**, 100
  Kampfgeschwader 44 **16**
  Kampfgeschwader 53 **13**, 15
  Kampfgeschwader 55 **12**
  Kampfgeschwader 66 **35**
  Kampfgeschwader 76 **48**
  Kampfgeschwader 100 **39, 40**
  Kampfgeschwader 101 **36**
  Kampfgeschwader 153 20
  Kampfgeschwader 155 20
  Kampfgeschwader 200 **83**, 85, **89**
Kampfgeschwader zur besonderen Verwendung 105 78, 98
Kampfgruppe 88 **11, 56**
Kampfgruppe zur besonderen Verwendung 1 **76, 80**
Kursk offensive (1943) 62
Küstenfliegergruppe
  Küstenfliegergruppe 106 94, 113, **114**
  Küstenfliegergruppe 406 105
  Küstenfliegergruppe 706 **113**
  Kustenfliegergruppe 906 **92**
  Küstenfliegergruppe 906 **94**

L
Lehrgeschwader
  Lehrgeschwader 1 **28, 32**, 33, **33**
  Lehrgeschwader 2 **55, 63**
Lufttransportstaffel 5 84

M
Messerschmitt Me 264 42
Messerschmitt Me 323 *Gigant* 86–8
  Me 323A-1 86
  Me 323C 86
  Me 323D 86–7
  Me 323E 87
  Me 323F 87
Mewes, Reinhold 64
Minensuchgruppe 1 **108**
Mussolini, Benito 66, 81

N
Nachtjagdgeschwader 2 **22**
Nachtkette/Nahaufklärungsgruppe 15 **69**
Nachtschlachtgruppe 4 **89**
Nahaufklärungsgruppe 15 **69**
Netherlands, the
  Dornier Do 17 **22**
  Dornier Do 217 **24**
  Fieseler Fi 167 106, **106**
  Heinkel He 111 15
Nicolaus, Friedrich 63
North Africa
  Blohm und Voss BV 222 110
  Henschel Hs 126 **64**
  Henschel Hs 129 69, **70**
  Junkers Ju 52 **80**
  Junkers Ju 87 **57**, 60
  Junkers Ju 88 **33**
Norway
  Arado Ar 196 **103**
  Arado Ar 234 *Blitz* **48**
  Blohm und Voss BV 138 **107**, 108
  Blohm und Voss BV 222 110
  Blohm und Voss Ha 139 97
  Dornier Do 26 105
  Focke-Wulf Fw 200 *Kondor* 98, **99**
  Heinkel He 59 **92**
  Heinkel He 111 **11**
  Heinkel He 115 114
  Junkers Ju 88 **29, 34**
  Junkers Ju 188 **44, 46**

O
Operation *Barbarossa* (1941) 61, 93
Operation *Citadel* (1943) 61
Operation *Marita* (1941) 22
Operation *Steinbock* (1942) 39, **46**

INDEX

P
Poland
  Dornier Do 17 **21**
  Dornier Do 215 **23**
  Focke-Wulf Fw 189 *Uhu* **69**
  Henschel Hs 123 54
  Junkers Ju 87 56–7
  Junkers Ju 88 29

R
Reeski, Hans 47
Reitsch, Hanna 66
Rudel, Hans-Ulrich **62**

S
Schlachtgeschwader
  Schlachtgeschwader 1 55, 69, **70**
  Schlachtgeschwader 2 **62**
  Schlachtgeschwader 9 **70**
Schubert, Richard 110
Seeaufklärungsgruppe
  Seeaufklärungsgruppe 125 102, **102, 109, 112**
  Seeaufklärungsgruppe 126 **89, 93, 104**
  Seeaufklärungsgruppe 129 111
  Seeaufklärungsgruppe 130 **107**
Seenotstaffel/SBK XI **96**
Sicily **33**
Siebel Si 204 88–9
  Si 204A-1 88
  Si 204D-0 88, 89
  Si 204D-1 88, 89
  Si 204D-3 88
  Si 204E 89
Sonderkommando **47,** 49
Spanish Civil War
  Dornier Do 17 20
  Fieseler Fi 156 *Storch* 65
  Heinkel He 59 92
  Heinkel He 111 10, **11**
  Henschel Hs 123 54
  Henschel Hs 126 63
  Junkers Ju 52 76
  Junkers Ju 86 17
  Junkers Ju 87 56, **56**
Stahl, Peter **32**
Stukageschwader
  Stukageschwader 2 **60, 61**
  Stukageschwader 5 **60**
  Stukageschwader 51 **57**
  Stukageschwader 76 58
  Stukageschwader 165 **54**

V
Versuchskommando fur Panzerbekampfung **35**
Versuchsverband Oberbefehlhaber der Luftwaffe 49
Vogt, Richard 72, 107, 110, 115

Y
Yugoslavia 20

Picture Credits

PHOTOGRAPHS:
AirSeaLandPhotos: 7, 8, 16, 18, 46, 51, 52, 71, 74, 81, 85, 90, 99, 114, 116
Amber Books/Aerospace: 6, 8, 11, 20, 25–45 all, 49, 57, 68, 77, 83, 87 all, 96, 104, 109

ARTWORKS:
Amber Books/Aerospace: 10, 13 top, 14/15, 17, 30/31, 32 top, 41, 44, 47, 51, 54, 55, 58/59, 64, 65, 67–72 all, 78/79, 80 bottom, 82, 89 all, 94, 96, 100/101
David Bocquelet: 11, 12 both, 13 bottom, 16, 19–21 all, 22 top, 23–27 all, 56, 57, 60–62 all
Vincent Bourguignon: 118–121 all
Ed Jackson – artbyedo.com: 39, 40, 42, 43, 46, 48–50 all, 63, 66, 73, 76, 80 top, 83–86 all , 92, 93, 95, 97–99 all, 102–115 all
Murilo Martins: 5, 22 bottom, 29 both, 32 bottom, 33–38 all